Carole A. Cobb, Ph.D.

The Nature Of The Journey

From There To Here

Xulon
PRESS

www.xulonpress.com

Now the LORD had said to Abram:
"Get out of your country,
From your family
And from your father's house,
To a land that I will show you.
I will make you a great nation;
I will bless you
And make your name great;
And you shall be a blessing.
I will bless those who bless you,
And I will curse him who curses you;
And in you all the families of the earth
shall be blessed."
Gen. 12:2-3

*"For unto whomsoever much is given,
of him shall much be required;" Luke 12:48b*

DEDICATION

In Memory of

My mother, Dorothy A. Cobb, who did not get to see me as an adult;

My grandparents, Cora & Sanford Turner, who helped me become one; and

My father, Robert 'Amos' Cobb, who stood in the gap and gave me the courage to be me.

My Eternal Love,
Carole

ACKNOWLEDGEMENTS

I give reverence to GOD, the Father, who has been and will always be my guiding light.

I give thanks to:

- My family for just being my family;
- Kavanaugh, my confidant and a woman of virtue, who has been my sounding board for over thirty years with whom I have shared my joy and my pain;
- Dr. Walter Malone, Jr. and First Lady Sandra Malone, of Canaan Christian Church, under whose spiritual leadership and friendship I began to develop an 'up close and personal' relationship with my heavenly Father; and
- Dr. Beverlin Hammett, a vessel of honor and a living epistle who has a heart after God.

I give a very special thanks to each of you who have thought enough of me to read my book. I pray that as you read it, the Holy Spirit will give you the peace that I found as I wrote it.

Agape'
Carole

TABLE OF CONTENTS

—⟋⟍⟋⟍—

Plant the Word – Grow in Love – Live in Faith

PREFACE

※※※

---

*When you remember what God brought you
through the last time, you can trust Him for
the now and the future for "Jesus Christ is
the same yesterday, today, and forever",
Hebrews 13:8.*

The men and women of God who had a profound
impact on my spiritual development through the
word-seeds they deposited were: Miss Virginia from
my childhood; Mrs. Cora Turner, my grandmother;
Bishops G.E. Patterson, Noel Jones, Kenneth Ulmer,
and T.D. Jakes; Pastors Dr. Walter Malone, Jr.,
Jentezen Franklin, Bayless Conley, and Jacquelyn
McCullough; and Drs. Creflo Dollar, Claudette
Copeland, Charles Stanley, and Betty Price. Some
of them planted, others watered, and God gave the
increase. Thank You, God, for these chosen vessels
who have been pliable enough to allow the Holy
Spirit to use them as conduits for the edification of

Your people. Bless them and help them to always be the spiritual leaders You created them to be.

The Nature of The Journey is one of continuous spiritual development where the only constant is change. As we go forth in ministry, God is constantly stretching us, increasing our capacity, so that we may walk worthy of our calling. He has entrusted each of us with the power of our destiny, through the Blood of Jesus Christ and The Word, to go after what He purposed in us before the foundations of this world. My heart's desire is not only that I become who God has called me to be, but also that I remain bold, steadfast, and unshakable in His Word as He releases me into my divine destination. I desire this for you as well.

I humbly invite you to travel with me through my faith journey. At the end of each Chapter, I share with you *The Nugget* from that leg of The Journey. It is my sincere prayer that, along the way, you will glean a greater degree of knowledge and reverence of God's ways, and the love He has so freely given each of us in the form of His Son, Jesus the Christ. May you become rich in wisdom and wealthy in understanding.

The Nature of The Journey – from there to here was delicately scripted by the Holy Spirit to provide a source of strength and encouragement for those who may find (or have found) themselves in situations that seem unbearable or unending. Realizing that all will not understand my entire journey, I am confident that each of you will recognize yourself in at least one of my experiences. No matter where you are on your journey of faith, just know that God is not a respecter of persons. So be strong and of good courage for, if the Holy Spirit has not yet pulled you out of the fire, He has stepped in it with you.

> *"Heart and soul, body and mind, but the very essence of our existence is spirit. What is it about the human spirit that produces the courage and the strength to beat insurmount-able odds, to survive and endure despite unbelievable circumstances? Our spirit embodies the very essence of our existence. We believe that it has been handed down from generation to generation beginning in Africa, the Motherland, where for eons, we believe the Creator heard us when we cried, saw us when we faulted and helped us along the way. And now, more than ever, it is time for us to get back in touch with the spirit that lives inside us all. Because without it we are less than whole but with it there is nothing we cannot overcome, for the very essence of our existence is spirit".*

Sounds of Blackness/Time for Healing, 1997

The Nugget: Nothing Just Happens!!!

PROLOGUE

"For I know the plans I have for you,"
declares the LORD, "plans to prosper you
and not to harm you, plans to give you hope
and a future", Jeremiah 29:11 (NIV).

"That's because I know you will make it. I don't have to worry about you like I do the others," answered my Grandmother whom I called Mom. From the age of fourteen, these were the words that I heard many times from her. However, it wasn't until *The Journey* that I really understood what she meant and how she could say them with such assurance.

This Journey has taught me that *here* is not a place or a destination – you won't be able to find it on MapQuest.com nor will On-Star get you *here*. It is a relevant term that is solely dependent upon one's point of reference; where one is in the spirit-realm at any given point and time. Each of our journeys may be similar in nature but no two are the same. This book walks you through *my* journey – *from there to here* – in search of purification, in search of righteousness, and in search of holiness. It tells of the preparation – periods from deconstruction through reconstruction – that was necessary for me to become empowered to move beyond just "naming it and claiming it" to faith-corresponding action. I learned to *apply* my faith in order to *"go in"* and possess the land that God had already promised me as my inheritance.

> *"Moses My servant is dead. Now therefore, arise, go over this Jordan, you and all this people, to the land which I am giving to them—the children of Israel. Every place that the sole of your foot will tread upon I have given you, as I said to Moses", Joshua 1:2-3.*

This journey of faith has left an indelible impression on me. My eyes have been opened to a whole new dimension of spiritual fortitude. I have learned that it is not what *I see* that counts but what *God says*. I have learned to see myself the way God sees me.

> *Thank You, Father, for waiting on me.*

Life's Journey

*Created as uniquely different as each drop of
dew
We are put on this earth to carry out a task or
two.*

*From the very first breath that we take
To the very last step that we make;
We are guided and nurtured by loving hands
Divinely protected from the wickedness of man.*

*Soon we spread our wings in search of nobility
Venturing into a world of challenges and
uncertainty.
Along our way we acquire wisdom and
understanding;
realizing our dreams and constantly planning.*

*We soon learn to appreciate our fellow being;
We learn to appreciate the world we are seeing.
We know the time we spend cannot be measured
For the gift of life is a priceless treasure.*

*We live...we love...we learn...we grow;
Changing with time as seasons come and go.
And soon we become like the wise oak tree,
Standing tall and eternally free.*

Carole A. Cobb, 1992

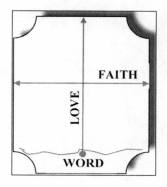

Plant the Word – Grow in Love – Live in Faith

PART ONE: Getting Established In God's Word

"Now may our LORD Jesus Christ Himself, and our God and Father, who has loved us and given us everlasting consolation and good hope by grace, comfort your hearts and establish you in every good word and work".
2 Thessalonians 2:16-17

Chapter One

In Retrospect

—◦◦◦—

"...Believe in the LORD your God, and you shall be established; believe His prophets, and you shall prosper", 2 Chronicles 20:20.

Understanding one's own miraculous creation is an important asset if one is to understand his or her journey. Because we were made in His image and in His likeness, through Christ our possibilities are limitless. However, this description does not pertain to our physical image but rather to the spiritual and moral components of who we are.

During my time of self-reflection, I began to ask myself a series of questions in order to ascertain this season. How have I become the person I am? What persons had the most influence in my life? What events had the greatest impact on my life? How did

I develop the attitude I now have? What do I value about myself? What do I value about life? Do I really see myself as God sees me? If not, why not?

One of the challenges of being children of God is living a life that is different and one that deserves to be taken seriously. This journey is not a destination but a continuous process of spiritual development containing hills and valleys; triumphs and trials; and many unforeseen detours and obstacles along the way. However, as you follow Jesus, one day at a time, He will keep you right in the center of God's will. Just remember that *no weapon formed against you shall prosper* (Isaiah 54:17) and that *you can do all things through Christ who strengthens you* (Phil. 4:13). So hold tight to the idea that God has chosen you to be a people for Himself, for you are a special treasure.

As with any journey, it cannot be completed alone. God longs to help us, support us, and give us vision as we thirst for and grow closer to Him. God promises that we will be blessed beyond measure for following the instructions in His Word. So that you can make the connection as to how I got *from there to here*, let me begin at the beginning.

In 1992, after fourteen years with the Detroit Public Schools I moved to Saginaw, MI to take an Assistant Principal position in Saginaw Township Community Schools. I became the first Administrator of color; the irony was bitter sweet. It was an honor to be the first to represent, but it was sad that it took until 1992 for this to happen. I thank God for His favor and will share the details of that experience in my next book.

The hardest test of faith I had ever experienced occurred the next year. In 1993 I lost my sixteen-year-old nephew, Joey, to heart failure. He was my oldest sister's son who lit up any room he entered with his brilliant smile and warm personality. Joey was a governor's scholar, a 6'2" all-star athlete, and an honor student. He attended church on a regular basis and dreamed of going to college and becoming an attorney. One day after practice he went home and sat down on the couch to eat his fruit and cottage cheese. He gently closed his eyes and went to sleep. When his Mom came home, she told him to get up and get ready for bed, not knowing that he had made his transition to be with the Father. Joey was so well loved that we had to use the high school gymnasium to hold his funeral. Students from seven counties came to bid him farewell. In his honor, the town even named the street in front of the school 'Joey Bumpous Avenue' – now that's love!

Joey's death was so unexpected; it ripped a hole in the heart of each of my family members – a hole we thought could never be repaired. We all dealt with it in our own way, but I was alone in Saginaw when I got the call. All I could do was bury my face deep in my pillow to keep from frightening my neighbors in the surrounding apartments as I moaned and wept uncontrollable. I had no one there to console me – family or friend; I felt so alone. Everyone else was back home and could comfort each other. No one was there to hold me as I cried my heart out to God asking Him time and time again why He had let this happen.

The next morning I was in a total state of depression; I didn't feel like getting out of bed. As I was lying there in a semi-state of consciousness I remembered talking with God. I told him that it didn't seem fair; what had Joey done? He was a good kid with a bright future; why take him? God did not answer me; at least I could not hear him through my pain. After two days of wallowing in self-pity, a sobering thought rose up in my spirit – what must his parents and his sister be going through? All I could do was fall on my knees and begin to pray, asking God for forgiveness, guidance, and strength. I remembered reading a Scripture from Isaiah 30:15, "If you will be calm and trust me, you will be strong". But because I didn't know how, I had to ask the Father in his great glory to give me the power to be strong inwardly through his Spirit.

After I got home I never had an opportunity to grieve openly as I had wanted because I knew I had to be strong in the faith in order to provide comfort to help my family, especially Joey's mother. I had to be the steadfast Christian I had claimed I was – they needed to see my light, my hope; they needed to see me be of good courage. Sandy, Joey's mom, asked me to go with her to the funeral home to view his body. After we saw him, she was displeased with his dull, grayish skin-tone; so was I. Since Joey had a radiant, dark-chocolate completion, she wanted him to look as natural as possible. Very unexpectedly, she asked *me* to redo his makeup. I didn't know what to say so I said nothing, but as difficult as it would be I knew I had to do it.

Even though the pain of it all rushes back right now and tears stream down my face as I recall our loss, that time alone with Joey was actually quite therapeutic. I remember reliving precious memories we had shared while he was but a toddler; I even got a chance to tell him some things I had not taken the opportunity to share with him before. I thanked God for our time together and for giving me the strength to get through this.

Nearing the completion of my third year working for the Township, I decided it was time to give back to the university that had given me so much. I knew I would have to take a substantial pay cut; none-theless, I resigned from my position as Assistant Principal, moved to Frankfort, KY, and took an Assistant Professorship at Kentucky State University in its undergraduate Teacher Education Program. My second year, I added the responsibility of being Director of Service Learning. My third year there, the Vice President of Academic Affairs asked me to take an Interim position as her Assistant Vice President (AVP), second in line to the President. This proved to be a six-month assignment during which I served as Co-chair of our Freshman Recruitment and Retention Task Force.

In 1997, just when my heart had finally begun to mend from losing Joey, I lost my oldest brother, Ronnie, to throat cancer. He was 45. The difference this time was that I had had an opportunity to visit with him two days before his death, and I wasn't alone when we got the news of his transition. I was at home with my family.

At the end of that academic year I moved to Louisville, KY and took an Associate Professorship at Bellarmine University in its School of Education (SOE). I joined Canaan Christian Church under the spiritual leadership of Dr. Walter Malone, Jr. and First Lady Sandra. I met them the year before when they came to Frankfort, and Dr. Malone was our keynote speaker for The Dr. Martin Luther King, Jr. Memorial Program. After I heard him deliver his message, I told him that if I ever moved to Louisville, I would join his church. Two years later, I was there. Canaan proved to be a place that embraced me as its own; a place where the Word was being rightly divided and I could grow spiritually. God placed me in a caring and loving church family, and connected me with two pillars of salt, Rev. Dianne Brown and Sister Annie White, who became my friends and my confidants. He knew I would need them to get through what was ahead of me. During my three-year period at Bellarmine, the regional 'premiere' Catholic University, my faith would truly be tested and my trust in God strengthened.

September 2000 marked the beginning of a series of events that would test the very essence of my being. My 10 year-old-niece, Cierra, was in a car accident with her two younger siblings. They came out with minor injuries, but Cierra later died in the hospital from internal injuries sustained in the accident. Five months later, in February 2001, my 27 year-old-nephew, Emanuel, lost his life in a motorcycle/car accident; the driver ran the stop sign. In June of that same year, my father succumbed to prostate cancer. It was only by God's grace that we didn't lose our minds. Our faith was the only thing that kept us going. As I look back over that time period, I take comfort in the joy of having had them in my life... even for just a while.

On the heels of these personal tragedies, I had to battle professionally to retain the position of Graduate Director at Bellarmine University in which I had served for the past year and a half. In an abbreviated version, when it came time for The School of Education to make this an official position, the Dean of Education did not want me to have it; her preference was a recently hired, recently degreed, young, ambitious Assistant Professor and a former Bellarmine graduate who was not of the darker persuasion. This was a secondary certification program and her training was in elementary. Not only did my qualifications and experience far surpass hers, I was the one who had researched, written, and submitted the proposal to the State Dept. of Education for approval. Even after the faculty voted on who they wanted to be placed in that position – a nine to two vote in my favor – the Dean overruled it and received full support of her decision from the Provost.

I tried on many occasions to reason with them concerning the injustice of this decision, but to no avail. You see, the Graduate Director would have to work closely with the Dean and be a part of the major decision-making process concerning the direction of the School. I surmised they believed I wasn't the 'best fit' based on several factors: 1) There were occasions when I had taken a stand and spoken out against the status quo when it went against what I believed to be right concerning the admissions policy, treatment of students of color, and programmatic decisions; 2) I had not come from the 'Louisville community' nor had I graduated from Bellarmine; and lest I forget, 3) I was of the darker hue...there were only seven African-American professors on the entire campus of this 'premiere regional Catholic Institute' and none were or had ever been a Director. During a candid conversation, one of my African-American colleagues told me the expectation was that "I was supposed to be *quietly* honored that I had been hired to teach there". Sure, they needed my expertise and my ethnicity but they did not want my spirit, the very essence of who I was and still am today.

In August of 2001, after consulting an attorney, I filed a discrimination lawsuit and resigned from Bellarmine University because it had become a hostile work environment. I won't disclose the intricate details or events that spun from this stop on my journey, but from my experience, it was a place where institution-alized racism ran rampant and where hidden biases abound. As time progressed, a very prominent and well-respected member of the 'Bellarmine community' shared with me that I had been blacklisted and was being secretly ostracized throughout the regional post-secondary community because I had "dared to sue Bellarmine". This proved to be true as it became increasingly difficult to find a job in my field even with my qualifications and all of my experiences. I learned one thing from this experience: Though life may not always be fair, it is what it is.

As I reflect on that time period in my life, the signs of injustice and inequality were there at the start. From the struggle to get on par with the salary of my colleagues after my first year probation ended, to getting institutional support in order to attend conferences and present on behalf of *their* University, up to this lawsuit ordeal. From August through October of 2001 I was unemployed and not eligible for any benefits, yet still had a mortgage, a car payment, and all of the other bills that came with the two. From November to August of 2002 I was underemployed, working as a substitute teacher in Jefferson County schools and making one-third of the money I had previously made. As David said in 2 Samuel 22:7, "In my distress I called upon the LORD, and cried out to my God; He heard my voice from His temple, and my cry *entered* His ears". Again, He proved himself strong. I had fallen five months behind in bill payments and had not yet been forced into foreclosure, nor had my car been repossessed!

In the end, all of this proved to be another pivotal period in my spiritual development. It drew me closer to my Canaan family and caused me to cleave to the Father, to snuggle up in His arms and find the comfort I so desperately needed. I began to search like never before for understanding and peace through His Word about what was happening in my life. I was led to go on my first real *spiritual* fast during which time these Scriptures continuously resounded in my spirit: "The LORD *is* my rock and my fortress and my deliverer;

"I am more than a conqueror"; and "the God whom I serve will deliver me". They had literally come to life for me and liberated me from my situation, my hurt, and my unforgiving attitude. After months and months of depositions and mediation, I was able to let go of the lawsuit and totally rest in God. I wanted whatever He had for me, not the 'stuff' placed in front of me designed to get me get off course. I intended to get the blessings He promised me and refused to forfeit my anointing for immediate gratification.

Know that God is aware of your situation. Within every problem, test, or trial is an opportunity for God to teach us more about His faithfulness. Don't give up. Keep *faithin' forward* no matter what. 2001 was the year I realized that God was trying to take me somewhere. It was then that I vowed to keep my eyes on where I was going. I wanted to demonstrate to Him how thankful I was for walking with – sometimes carrying – me through the [then] roughest time in my life. At times this was difficult, but His grace was sufficient and His strength was made mighty in my weakness. As Dr. Charles Stanley advises, "establish yourself in His Word and He will give you the perspective to face trails, the wisdom to make decisions in the days ahead, and the faith to endure". In retrospect, I understand that these trials were the beginning of how I got established in God's Word.

The Nugget: *The quicker you learn the lesson, the quicker you will pass the test.*

To Be Righteous Is To Walk In Faith.

Chapter Two

Submission In The Mist Of Transition

―∽∾∿―

"Purge me with hyssop, and I shall be clean:
wash me, and I shall be whiter than snow.
Create in me a clean heart, O God; and renew
a right spirit within me", Psalm 51:7, 10.

From the time I had arrived in Louisville, I had become active in its community working closely with the Jefferson County Public Schools (JCPS) in their Equity Office and with the Urban League's Campaign for African-American Achievement. But even those connections did not make my job search any easier until August of 2002, one year after the Bellermine episode, when God gave me favor with Dr. Bonnie Marshall. I met and briefly worked with her in 1997 at Kentucky State in its Teacher Education

Program; neither of us knew that five years later we would work together again. A nationally known and well-respected educator, Dr. Marshall had just retired from JCPS and took the position as Director of Spalding University's Alternative Route Teacher Certification Masters' Program. One day I saw her in the lobby of JCPS' Central Office; in casual conversation she asked me what I was doing. My response was 'looking for a job'. She (and everyone else) had heard about the 'Bellarmine Affair' but my spirit knew that she recognized the rippling affect it had had on my professional career. She wished me well and we went our separate ways.

Two weeks later I applied for an adjunct position at Spalding, not remembering that Dr. Marshall now worked there. When she heard that I had applied she recommended to the Dean that I become her Assistant Director with teaching as part of my responsibilities. I learned that they were in the beginning stages of establishing their Master's Program, and wanted to take advantage of my expertise and the work I had done for Bellermine…look at how God was working on my behalf! Dr. Marshall was a Godsend, both personally and professionally. With over thirty-five years of experience in the field she had a lot of information from which I could glean to expand my expertise. Though the position was a temporary one, God had allowed me to find my MAAT – my balance – again, at least for a while.

Six months later, my soul became restless again as I questioned what I was to do with my life after this assignment: What is going to happen after this year is over? Should I change my profession again? Could I now go to law school, which was my original desire before God changed my plans? You see, my undergrad degree was in Criminal Justice Education. During my senior year I had passed the Law School Admissions Test (LSAT) with a high score, and had gotten accepted into the University of Michigan Law School. That summer, after graduation, I took a job with Detroit Public Schools working with low socioeconomic juniors and seniors. I took a one-year deferment from entering law school that turned into a twenty-four year career in education.

Weeks of deliberation (with myself) went by. I grew impatient waiting for God to be God so I did what many of us do; I injected my will. *I decided* this was my pass to go to law school. After all, I wasn't tied to anything or anybody. I had been celibate for six years, had no children, was on the brink of having to sell my house – there was nothing to keep me in Louisville except my church family, and they would understand my decision.

My impatience had given room for the enemy to step in. I got on the Internet and researched the Law Schools I wanted to attend. I needed to choose one in the area where I wanted to live, near the water. I narrowed my choices to Duke University, the University of Richmond, and the University of Virginia; and, oh yes, just in case, the University of Kentucky and the University of Louisville. I did not really study for the LSAT because I did quite well when I took it before. I was confident I could "figure it out" by using my cognitive intellect and applying my years of practical experience. Besides, I had always been in the top of my classes, had earned my Ph.D., was quite an accomplished educator, and was well established in the community. My mindset was that I would take it, and even if I just did okay, I would still get accepted into one of these law schools.

As the weeks went by I prepared mentally and emotionally to carry out *my* plan to leave Kentucky for law school, yet I had not prepared myself for *God's* plan. Sure, I had asked God to let His will be done; I had asked that He would shut every door to my plan if this was not what He wanted me to do – but I didn't actually mean it! My advice to you is to be careful for what you ask. Despite the fact that I had graduated Magna Cum Laude and had amassed a number of honors and awards, I was denied admission to every one of those law schools. In essence, their letters all said the same thing, "because of an unusual amount of applicants this year, there was no room for me". The first three rejections that came were from the University of Richmond, followed by Duke University, and then the University of Virginia. I was disappointed but that was okay. I still had two aces to play (so I thought), the University of Kentucky and the University of Louisville. As a Kentucky resident, I was supposed to be given admission preferences. *My* plans were to do my first year at one of these schools and then transfer. "Not so," said the LORD. All of a sudden I heard this resounding noise…Bam …Bam…Bam…Bam…Bam! God had taken me up on my request and had shut every one of those doors. Now that got my attention for real!

I was crushed and at a loss. After all, God's Word said to "take delight in the LORD, and He will give you the desires of your heart". Well, I truly delighted myself in Him and my desire was to go to law school; however, there is another Scripture that says "But seek ye first the Kingdom of God and all His righteousness, and all these things shall be added unto you". I had inquired of God but in my hurt and confusion, I had not *diligently* sought Him. I realized that I was trying to go ahead of God while he was trying to give me direction. Desperately in need of His guidance, I ran back to Him and asked for forgiveness. I did what I should have done months earlier – I fasted and prayed with expectancy in my heart. Then Psalm 46:1 rose up in my spirit, "God is our refuge and strength, a very present help in trouble". Being the loving, merciful, and just God that He is, He forgave me of my arrogance.

In a quiet, still voice He whispered to me, "I have a greater work for you. What I have for you to do you cannot do in Kentucky, but I will tell you when to go. Your work is to be international; you are to influence leaders, and I have already deposited in you everything you need. I now want you to use all of your gifts, talents, skills, and abilities that you have used in the world for the expansion of my Kingdom." I did not know exactly what this meant or the scope of what it would entail; however, I did know that the Holy Spirit would instruct me along the way. As time went on, the revelation became quite clear. Preparation would be a requirement for this transition; however, it would not be instantaneous.

According to John 15:2-4, I had to be pruned. Jesus said, "Every branch in Me that does not bear fruit He takes away; and every branch that bears fruit, He prunes, that it may bear more fruit. You are already clean because of the word which I have spoken to you. Abide in Me, and I in you. As the branch cannot bear fruit of itself, unless it abides in the vine, neither can you, unless you abide in me." God was trying to teach me about submission, how to go *under* the mission – His mission – with blind obedience. This would be the first leg of my faith journey.

While on earth, Jesus' message was 'believe in me'. Amazingly, when we do, He opens us up to receive great power after we submit our will to God's will, as He did during His journey to the Cross. I believe the greatest pain Jesus felt before going to the Cross, was the pain of having to fit His divine omnipotence into man's finiteness. Jesus, being the outward expression of the essence of God, had/has *all* power, yet He told the Father, "Nevertheless not My will, but Thine will be done". Jesus went on to endure much verbal and physical persecution before completing His earthly mission, and committing His Spirit unto the Father's hands at Calvary. The Roman Centurion Guard, Longinus, wanted to make sure Jesus was dead, so he pierced Him in the side with his spear. He had no idea of the power he had just unleashed! *Immediately* the Blood – the living water – flowed forth and all of heaven was opened. Jesus' power was released and made available for all who would believe and submit; to everyone who would trust in God's Son.

All believers have had or will have a 'spear' thrust into their side as a way for the power of God to be released and manifested in their lives. I have discerned that the spear that was thrust into my side, during this time, was meant to unleash the power of the Holy Spirit in me; to prosper me and not to harm me; to teach me how to submit and commit my will to do the will of my Father. Through this journey of discovery, *from there to here*, I learned that all struggling is not because of sin. Sometimes God has to get us to a place where we can hear only His voice, so He can save us from ourselves. He allows each of us to see our frailties – our true selves – so that we draw nearer to Him. So in my times of pain and struggle, I had to remember that God was using my circumstances, *my spear,* to forge my character and enshrine my gifts. It was during these times that I snuggled closer to the Father and deepened my relationship with Him. It was through my struggles I learned to persevere; maturing in spirit, in character, and in integrity. I believe that God allows struggles in our lives to keep us grounded and focused on Him; to prevent us from becoming prideful when He blesses us with success. God resists the proud, but gives grace to the humble; thusly, reminding us that He is The Source of all that we accomplish, and that apart from Him we can do nothing.

God lavished His grace on every one of us through the person of His Son, Jesus the Christ, and the key to accessing that grace is faith. *"For in it the righteousness of God is revealed from faith to faith; as it is written, 'The just shall live by faith'"*. When

I submitted to the Father I received an increased capacity of faith that surpassed my ability to see in the natural, and my whole life began to change. I learned how to submit, and finally knew what Kavanaugh meant when she told me to "just rest in His presence". From the wisdom of Dr. Stanley, "True peace is not external, not dependent upon the environment. It is internal, springing from your innermost being. This peace comes only through the inner presence of the Prince of Peace, Jesus Christ. He can settle your spirit and mind, regardless of external disarray."

God, the creator of time and space, made us after His image, blew breath into our bodies, and endowed us with His Spirit. As believers, we are now a part of His wonderful family. God has adopted us into the royal priesthood, and called us to a higher place of praise. Tokunboh Adeyemo said, "The church today is one mile long, but only one inch deep". As spiritually minded leaders of God, we are charged with changing this 'norm' within the church so that the world can see us moving with excellence: one mind, one body, one spirit. We need to be more in Christ and less in Church. However, in order to move, we have to bring closure to the old things of man before we can begin the new things of God.

Our forward progress is sometimes hindered because we don't submit to the voice of the Spirit – especially when He speaks through others – even when we know what we have heard was right. The Holy Spirit intercedes on our behalf for God's will to be superimposed over ours, but if our minds are not made up to cooperate, then to submit our will for His is hard. Nonetheless, even when we choose the hard way, God can still use our stubbornness to mold us into the men and women He created us to be. I had to totally submit my will, even in the midst of my transition, in order for Jesus' fullness to come forth through me. True submission, a joyful acquiescence in all the providence of God, consists of a spirit of universal obedience to the whole will of God, because it is His will. "Submit yourselves therefore to God. Resist the devil and he will flee from you. Draw near to God and He will draw near to you", James 4:7-8.

The Nugget: Only by submitting to the LORD's leadership, through the Spirit, do we find wholeness and direction.

Submission Is A Faith-Act Of Obedience.

Chapter Three

Transformation

"I beseech you therefore, brethren, by the mercies of God, that ye present your bodies a living sacrifice, holy, acceptable unto God, which is your reasonable service. And be not conformed to this world, but be ye transformed by the renewing of your mind, that ye may prove what is that good and acceptable and perfect will of God", Romans 12:1-2.

"Since the beginning of time man has tried to conquer the universe not realizing that when he conquers himself the universe is his," (Carole A. Cobb, 1995). As it is written, "In the beginning, God created...And God saw that it was good. Then God said, 'Let Us make man in Our image, according to Our likeness; let them have dominion over the fish of the sea, over the birds of the air, and over the cattle, over all the earth and every living thing that moves on the earth'". Man had it made! The one thing he didn't have was dominion over himself as evidenced by his fall in the Garden. It is easy to surmise that before man can operate in dominion over the universe, he must operate in dominion over himself. Subsequently, we cannot operate in the dominion God has given us unless it is operating within us.

Transformation can readily be defined as change in form, appearance, nature, and character. In biological genetics, transformation is the transfer of material from one cell to another resulting in a hereditary change in the recipient cell. In spiritual genetics, as believers, we are the recipient cells of God's DNA and should no longer be conformed by the patterns of this world but through The Blood be transformed *by the renewing of our minds, that we may prove what is that good and acceptable and perfect will of God.* Dr. Cindy Trimm once wrote, "As a spiritual being created in the image of God (Gen. 1:26), our spiritual genes hold the creative power to frame our personal world by the thoughts and words we think and speak, which are divine tools given for our creative use". However, it doesn't stop there.

Each of us must allow this spiritual infusion of The Blood to penetrate and transform our hearts. In Hebrew, the word for heart is *'leb'*. Our heart is the center of our entire being and determines the course of our lives. Therefore, we must guard our heart above all else for it is *the closest of secret communion with God (Eph. 5:19).* One of the greatest joys as believers is to have Jesus ever near, dwelling in our hearts; and as believers, our thirst for the knowledge of Christ should never be satisfied. We should continuously long to drink deeply of His Spirit, to experience deeper manifestations of His presence. We should yearn "that Christ may dwell in our hearts by faith"; that He may abide in or take up residency within us. It is in His 'dwelling' that we establish and continuously fortify our relationship with God the Father. It is in His 'abiding' that our faith becomes stronger; our love for Christ becomes unquenchable.

Transforming our mind and heart is not an easy task and can be a challenging and painful process, yet a necessary one. We can't have new blessings and handle them in old ways. It takes courage to shine a light into the dark corners of our lives because we have to become vulnerable and transparent to others. It is only when we learn to forgive ourselves for our missteps; to let go of those things that are holding us captive; and to break free from the bondage of yesterday that we can renew our lives and re-position ourselves for what God has for us NOW. Only then can we find joy in the opportunities that await us in the present.

Nearly every time I asked God what I was supposed to do relative to the assignment He gave me, He sent my answer through the preached word. Through my intimate relationship with God and my spirit of discernment it was confirmed. Like many of you, I didn't show my inner sphere to many people because I didn't like being in a state of vulnerability to my enemy friends, known and unknown. The strength that I displayed was what I needed to take care of myself and survive within my environments; it was a strength I could only get as I walked in the light of the knowledge of God. Now, that I understand my uniqueness and who I have been called to be, I embrace it and realize that it is only when I let my light shine on others that I can then see my own God-like reflection.

We know that prisms of light come in varying spectrums, from a dull yellow to a vibrantly brilliant white, depending on the time and care taken to shape them. As believers, we must reflectively use care and caution to shape our lives as we operate in this world but not of this world. This introspective process is God's way of allowing us to filter out the 'dull' rays of hurt that hide life's true colors of joy, peace, and love in order to produce cleaner, whiter-looking light when forming our relationships with others. We are then able to see everything in our lives in a whole new light – God's color-enhanced, full-spectrum light illuminates our paths as we allow it to continue to shine even when we are in our dark places. So, as a faithful warrior, I must stand ready to do battle for whomever is in need – even in my time of need.

From the teachings of Pastor Malone, I knew that God's promises would not be established in my life automatically. Yes, although I knew I had His divine protection, I also knew that I would have to do my part. I would have to participate in the process. Because I *believe* what God told me, I had to begin to exercise my faith by acting and speaking differently. As Dr. Dollar so eloquently put it, I had to *locate His promises in the Word* because everything starts with the Word. Then I had to *put the Word in my mouth* because our authority is in speaking God's Word. I began to call things as I wanted them to be, not as they were – speaking things into existence according to His Word. I began to frame my world with His Word (Heb. 11:3) because the laws of confession will work for anybody who will put them to work. And finally, I had to *meditate in the Word,* put it in my heart day and night, until the Word spoke back to me. It was then that I had a breakthrough; I became more confident in what was on the inside of me than what was on the outside of me. I was evolving into a living epistle, daily "walking out" the Word with faith-corresponding action and a Christ-like mindset. My faith had become a practical expression of my confidence in God and His Word. I had moved from knowing the Word to knowing the Life behind the Word. I was in a place where I trusted God completely – rooted in an unshakeable faith in the God of the Scriptures. I had now established myself in the Spirit!

After several months had past, God had not told me where I'd be going so I reminded Him – imagine that – of my love for water. I wanted to go to the east or west coast, Virginia Beach or San Diego, and live near an ocean. It seemed as if God just smiled and nodded His head. I knew absolutely no one in San Diego. On the other hand, I had a dear colleague, Landis, who lived in the Virginia Beach area so I contacted her. It just so happened that her organization had an open position, though not yet posted, for which I was qualified. It would afford me an opportunity to continue working with government officials and spearheading initiatives for the economic and educational empowerment of families and communities.

With the preliminaries behind me I flew out a day before my interview. I rented a car from the airport and decided to take a tour of the city before checking into the hotel. As I drove around in the area in which I would work, and possibly live, an uncomfortable feeling hit me in the pit of my stomach. I knew it was the Holy Spirit telling me that this was not what He had planned for me. Now what was I to do? It was too late to cancel my interview and return home; I had to go through with it. The interview went well. I was offered the job with full benefits and several administrative perks, yet I knew I had to pray about accepting the position because I wanted to stay in line with God's plans. Consequently, I asked for time to think about it. The day after I returned home I called Landis, told her that I could not accept the position, and apologized for any inconvenience I may have caused. Being a woman of faith herself, she understood.

This time I sought God *before* I sat out and asked Him if I could go to California, still wanting to be near the water. When He said, "Yes", I took this to mean San Diego because I remembered how beautiful it was the last time I visited. Mind you, I had no place to live, no job waiting for me, and I knew no one there; I was just willing to be obedient. I began to make preparations to put my house on the market, and move everything into storage except the essentials I would pack in my car for my cross-country journey – my laptop, printer, CD player, gospel and jazz CDs, micro-tape recorder, clothes, and toiletries. Like Abram, I was to make no provisions to return.

I made an appointment with my Pastor to share with him all that God had spoken to me. He knew that I had to have heard this from God because he knew the relationship I had with the Father. After Pastor Malone gave me his blessings, I told my family, my choir members, and then my church family my plans. The number of those who told me that I was 'brave' to just uproot my life and travel across country, by myself, without having a plan once I got to San Diego, surprised me. Some even admitted that they didn't know whether or not they could make this kind of sacrifice. What they didn't understand was that I wouldn't be alone; what they had forgotten was that His Word declares that *obedience is better than sacrifice*. I was just being obedient.

In the spirit, what they had actually told me was that they did not know whether they could trust God to that degree of obedience. During the time I had spent in the furnace at Bellarmine, I learned that partial obedience is disobedience; it had to be all or nothing. I suddenly realized that even though Christians operate in faith, some might not operate in trust. When we don't trust we stifle the blessings of God. Jeremiah 17:7 tells us "Blessed is the man who trusts in the LORD, and whose hope is the LORD". I believe that once we get past *religiosity*, move into spirituality, and establish a deep *relationship* with God, total obedience is not an option. In fact, it becomes one's desire to obey because obedience pleases God. It is a reflection of our faith. I had to learn not to judge them nor allow where they were in the spirit to hinder what God told me to do or where He told me to go. After all, I was the one who had asked God to use me.

The Word of God is an equipping tool; therefore, to continuously renew our minds we must meditate on the Scriptures day and night. As believers and followers of Christ, if we are to be the reality we say we are, we must turn our knowledge *about* God into knowledge *of* God. Let me use the analogy of a Pitcher, Cup, Saucer, and Plate to represent the dynamic ingredients in God's process for our spiritual transformation. As **The Pitcher** – the infinite Source of energy, direction, passion, love, and everything else we need for ministry – when God pours Himself into **The Cup** of our lives, transformation is inevitable. By His grace alone, this ongoing transformation spills onto **The Saucer**, the relationships of our lives, and then onto **The Plate**, the ministries to which God has called us. Our leadership then is an overflow of God's love, His character, and His power – of all of Himself that He is continuously pouring into the Cup of our lives. Our leadership, our obedience honors God as we fulfill His will for His church and for His people. And such efforts must be rooted in a leader's life-giving relationship with God. This can only happen when we know and live the Life behind the Word, allowing God to transform our minds by the daily renewing of our spirit.

My journey has taught me that faith should always lead to corresponding action because God is faithful to those who are faithful to Him. Faith entitles us to our inheritance. Ephesians 1:13-14 proclaims, "And you also were included in Christ when you heard the word of truth, the gospel of your salvation. Having believed, we were marked in him with a seal, the promised Holy Spirit, who is a deposit guaranteeing our inheritance until the redemption of those who are God's possession—to the praise of His glory." Because I am God's possession, I had faith enough to say what I believed even when I was in my Lo Debar (an Old Testament town in Gilead meaning a place of "no pasture"). If we don't believe what we say, God won't either. Besides, since God had promised me the desires of my heart, I knew He was repositioning me to receive a series of supernatural manifestations as my inheritance; therefore, I could not negate the process.

The Nugget: *Don't ask God to order your steps if you are not willing or ready to move your feet!*

Faith Is The Natural By-Product Of Our Relationship With Christ.

Plant the Word – Grow in Love – Live in Faith

PART TWO: My Wilderness Experience

"So Jesus answered and said, "Assuredly, I say to you, there is no one who has left house or brothers or sisters or father or mother or wife or children or lands, for My sake and the gospel's, who shall not receive a hundredfold now in this time—houses and brothers and sisters and mothers and children and lands, with persecutions—and in the age to come, eternal life. But many who are first will be last, and the last first."

Mark 10:29-31

Chapter Four

Separation

—◦∕◦∕◦—

*"By faith Abraham obeyed when he was
called to go out to the place which he would
receive as an inheritance. And he went out,
not knowing where he was going", Hebrews
11:8.*

To separate means to pull apart, to move away
from; to disengage; or to break free. Separation
is necessary for preparation for a faith journey. Make
sure your friends qualify for where God is taking
you; if not, let them go. I learned I could not gain
entry into the place where I was going, nor could I
obtain the stuff God had for me, until I unpacked the
seven-piece luggage set I had been carrying – this
included most of my friends. I had to learn that if *it*
wouldn't fit in my clothes bag and overnight carrying

case – no matter what the *it* was – I didn't need to take *it* with me. How could I not let go! After all, Moses gave up the riches of Egypt to follow God and Jesus the Christ gave up His life that I might live.

In order to make this journey, I had to totally rely on God as El Shaddai, God Almighty, the All Sufficient One in whom there is no lack. I had to fully understand that God wanted to bless me beyond measure. His intention was to provide for me in every way. My Father who owns the cattle on a thousand hills had everything in His heavenly storehouse that I would need. I would just have to make room to receive.

Many of us have been there. For those who have not, there will come a time when you will have to separate yourself from people *and* stuff in order to move into your place of promise, your place of blessing. You will give up pleasure for purpose. I had to realize that my security was in the *found* purpose of God and not the opinion of man. People, even family, will try to offend you, talk you out of your position, or lie you out of your posture. Therefore, be mindful of the people with whom you keep company. Make sure you only keep those around you that support you and remind you of *whose* you are and what your God-given purpose is.

On August 1, 2003 I hosted a Faith Journey Celebration in the all-purpose room of the Canaan Community Development Center. I did all the planning, hired a caterer and a DJ, and invited all of my closest friends and church family to celebrate with me what God was about to do in my life. We had a

ball! During the celebration I was given two proph-
ecies. Minister Eugene told me that everything and
everybody I needed would be waiting for me in
California. Rev. Dianne told me that I would have
a school of my own. Because my spirit bore witness
to what they both had spoken into my life, I believed
and received it and deposited both into the data bank
of my mind.

That night I slept in my house for the last time.
The next day I attended my last service as a choir
member and as a disciple of Canaan Christian
Church. That evening, before heading to San Diego,
I drove four hours south to bid my family farewell.
They all lived within a twenty-mile radius so my first
stop was Hickman, KY, then Union City, TN, and
then South Fulton, TN. On August 3rd I embarked
upon the journey that would change my life forever.

With the assistance of MapQuest.com, I strategically planned this 2,100-mile trip. In the early
1980's and 90's I drove continuously for eleven
hours, from Detroit to Hickman, stopping only for
gas and fast food. Being a little older and a lot wiser
now, I decided to divide this trip and treat each day
as if it was a workday. Each day I drove three and a
half hours, stopped for an hour lunch break, and then
drove another three and a half hours before eating
dinner and spending the night in a hotel in which I
had previously made reservations. I knew I would
never come this way again, at least not by myself nor
for the same reason, so I thought of this as a vaca-
tion. Wanting to enjoy all of the wonderful sites and
the beautiful landscape of God's country, to take it

all in, I took pictures and bought souvenirs at every stop. My longest stay at any one place was Sedona, AZ. Kent, one of my undergrad college roommates, told me how beautiful this place was, so I decided to treat myself to four days of rest and relaxation. She was absolutely right. It was simply breathtaking and so peaceful.

My second night there, the Holy Spirit tapped me on my shoulder and simply asked me, *"Now where are you really going?"* I was somewhat surprised because I was headed to San Diego and thought surely He knew that. Then the conversation came back to me that we had had concerning my move to California. God said that I should go to California, but *I* had chosen San Diego because that is where I wanted to live if I ever moved to California. So when I asked the Holy Spirit for clarity, He told me to go to Los Angeles (L.A.). Without hesitation I got on MapQuest.com again to plot my course. I picked up the phone and called Mark, another dear friend from my undergrad days, who lived in Whittier, about twenty-five minutes south of L.A. He had been trying to get me to move to California for the past ten years. He and his wife, Diane, had extended an open invitation to stay with them if I ever came. I decided it was time to take them up on it. I began telling him that I was in Sedona headed to San Diego until the LORD redirected me to Los Angeles. Before I could finish sharing my story he said, "Girl, what are you talking about. You're supposed to be here. You don't have any business in San Diego. Come on down. Di and I are going to Mexico this weekend. We'll just give you the keys and see you when we get back"...Now that's a true friend.

On August 15th I arrived at Mark and Diane's. They welcomed me with open arms; Mark hugged me as if I were his long-lost sister. They helped me take everything in, showed me how to work the alarm, gave me the keys, and they were off to Mexico. Wow! I had made it. This was the first time I realized the magnitude of what I had just done. I had just finished driving a 2100-mile faith journey across country. I stood in the middle of the hallway and began to praise God for my safe travels and for the promises He had made to me before releasing me from Kentucky. God had even set it up so that I could have the weekend in solitude to download my thoughts and process what He had just allowed me to do. How could I not love a God like this...He is so awesome!

I knew that eventually I would move to L.A. so I needed someone to show me around. I remembered that I had met Paul, the brother of Dianne, my friend in Louisville, when he had come to visit her a year ago. I called Di and she gave me his number. Paul proved to be a friend and a gentleman. He took me to different cultural events, the movie theatres, and out to dinner on many occasions. He even went to church with me, which was a wonder in itself because Paul is a Muslim. I enjoyed watching his body language as he processed the worship service.

The next three months proved to be another pivotal point in my spiritual development that helped me define what I believed in and stood for. God stretched me upwardly and outwardly. It was too late to try to get on at any of the Universities so I applied for a teaching position with the Los Angeles Unified School District (LAUSD) but was placed on a waiting list until what they call 'norm' day. The same was true for the other surrounding school districts so I was in a state of limbo. Even though I had not found a job and my savings was running low, I offered Mark and Diane some money to cover my living expenses. Of course they would not take anything. I believe they knew I would need it to make ends meet until I got a job, but were too kind to mention that. The truth is that I would have had more than enough to sustain me if, six weeks before I began my journey, I had not loaned a 'friend' $3,500 dollars to save her home from foreclosure. Yvette was an Independent Consultant and one of her clients had not yet paid her for her services. I had saved this money to take my trip in August but I felt her need was more urgent than mine. However, before loaning it to her, I stressed the necessity of getting my money back by August as I would need it for expenses once I got to California in case I didn't find a job right away. She assured me that she would pay it back by then…more than five years have passed and I have learned to count it all joy.

As my finances got tighter and tighter, I began to feel like I was in a vacuum. In my room I secretly cried every night, and often questioned God why He was allowing this to happen. I know I had done what He had told me to do, yet I was struggling on all fronts. In my desperation, I decided to do something

I said I would never do, apply for state assistance. After thinking about it, I asked myself, "Why not?" I had been a taxpayer all my adult life, a contributing citizen to society, and I felt I had a right. Well as it turned out, I couldn't receive general assistance or even get food stamps because I owned a car. I was told that if I sold my car, or didn't claim it on the form, I would qualify...how crazy was that! I knew this was just a temporary situation so that didn't make sense to me nor was I going to lie. Furthermore, if I sold my car, how would I get back and forth to work when I did get a job? How would I get back and forth to church? I was in a quandary. What was I to do?

I remembered what my Dad told me some time ago. He said, "Carole, always buy good jewelry, the real stuff. You never know when you may need to put it in hock." Because I never thought I would need to remember this advice, I didn't pay any attention to what he had said even though I loved and purchased only quality jewelry. By this time in my life, I had accumulated quite a bit of it; most had been custom-made. I ended up having to follow his advice and put most of my jewelry in pawn. (Some of it stayed there for three years, until my period of *Restoration*). Soon, even the money from that ran out. It was November and I still had not found a job. It took me a while to realize it, but now I was right where God wanted me, totally depended on Him. No one knew my pain – not Mark, not Kavanaugh, not even my family – because I never showed it nor shared it. I always had a smile on my face when I went to church and continued to speak affirmations and encouragement to others. I never stopped praising God or seeking His face. I would tithe on what little I had and I continued to fast and pray and read the Word. One day I ran across Psalm 27:14, "Wait and hope for and expect the LORD; be brave and of good courage and let your heart be stout and enduring. Yes, wait for and hope for and expect the LORD." That was when I received my peace in the mist of my circumstance.

A week later things began to manifest. I received a part-time job offer from UCLA to work in its Teacher Education Program, and then a full-time placement at Gage Middle School as its in-house staff developer/ faculty workshop facilitator. I really wanted to work at UCLA, but I knew I needed the salary and bene- fits a full-time job would provide. So, by default, I leaned toward Gage. That afternoon I received a call from LAUSD telling me to contact Hamilton High School for a computer science opening...all good things come in threes.

I went to an interview at Hamilton that Friday and to my surprise one of the Assistant Principal's brother was a graduate of Kentucky State, my Alma Mater. The interview went well, as I expected it to, because I went in prayed up and had already asked God to represent me with clarity of thought, articula- tion of tongue, and sincerity of spirit as I responded to their questions. They said they had several more interviews to conduct and would let me know within a week or so. I boldly told them, "That's fine, but I would like to have a chance to meet with the sub and the class a couple of days before I start in the position"...the Word tells us to speak those things that are not, as though they were, so I did. As they chuckled lightly I thanked them for the opportunity to interview and left.

As God would have it, that following Monday, the Assistant Principal called me and offered me the job! It would be a long-term sub position but I would start on November 17th. Later, in a discussion about expectations, he shared with me that next year they wanted me to give leadership to moving the Computer Science program up a level into a Business Management and Technology Magnet. By that time I would have taken and passed the CBEST which is a requirement for all California teachers. GOD IS S-O-O-O AWESOME. All this time I had kept in tough with my Canaan church family who constantly interceded to the Father on my behalf. I thank God for each of my faith-journeymen and prayer warriors for the prayers of the righteous do availeth much.

I had grown tired of searching for a church and was really ready to be rooted in good soil. I visited several churches in L.A. but was not led to join any of them. In a conversation with Kavanaugh, she asked me if I had visited The City. I had not. The irony of this was that I had forgotten The City was in my area even though its Pastor had come to Canaan, my church in Louisville, for the past two years, and delivered the opening message for our church conference. The following night was Wednesday's Bible study so I decided to go, not knowing that the Holy Spirit was waiting on me there. As soon as I took a seat He whispered, "This is where I want you planted; I have an assignment for you here". I could not image what it was nor did I ask because I knew He would tell me in His timing. My job was simply to obey when He did.

Under normal circumstances my daily trek from Whittier to Los Angeles was only a 25-minute drive; however, driving to and from work during rush hour consumed more than an hour of my time each way. Whoever named it 'rush hour' had a cruel sense of humor because 'rush' implies to move quickly – there was *nothin'* quick about the movement of this traffic! Even Detroit's traffic was never this congested. I was never one who enjoyed commuting. So after the second week, in faith, I began searching for a place in the city to live, somewhere close to my job. I had no more savings and had not made enough money to move into my own apartment, yet I knew God would come through as He always had.

The first week of December the Father gave me favor with Karen, a minister in the faith. Karen owned a transitional home for women who had been clean for 30 days, and needed a place where they could be orientated back into society to live productive lives. Though this was not my situation, after a church member told me she had a vacancy, I called Karen and asked for an appointment. After hearing my 'transitional' story Karen agreed to let me move in until I could save enough money and find my own place. She only charged me $400 a month and had just one stipulation: I would have to follow the rules of the house, i.e. no male company, no smoking or drinking of alcoholic beverages, and full participation in its upkeep. This was a reasonable request, especially since I wasn't dating and didn't smoke or drink. It was certainly fair that I help around the house. This was a whole new dynamic for me, but God had opened the door so I knew there had to be a purpose behind it.

The manager of the home lived down stairs while the residents all lived upstairs. I had a private bedroom and bathroom but the other three women in the house shared their living quarters and bathroom. We were all assigned sufficient kitchen cabinet shelves where we could store our food and dishes. We were also allocated our own shelf space in the refrigerator. There was a TV in the community room that the ladies were allowed to watch during scheduled TV time. There was a telephone in the office that was available for them by permission, but with a limited time per call. I was given permission to have my own TV and phone installed in my room. Downstairs was the living room, a dining area, another kitchen, a utility room with a washer and dryer, an extra bathroom for visitors and a small back room that was being converted to a study and computer room. There was a nice size deck in back and a gated parking area. Twice a month we had 'Double-Scrub day' where we each had a specific area of the house that we were responsible for 'scrubbing down'.

At first, even though I knew God had strategically placed me there, I was ashamed to tell anyone, including Mark and Paul, that I was staying in a transitional home because of the negative connotation that I had associated with it. Whenever we hung out, I would meet them at the location instead of letting them pick me up. Then I remembered a biblical reference that I had heard many times before, "...but for His grace, there go I". Humbled, I asked God to forgive my lack of gratitude. I blessed Him and thanked Him for putting it on Karen's heart to allow me to stay there. I even allowed both Mark and Paul to pick me up.

During the next several months I attended The City on a regular basis where the message was Word-based and well seasoned. I had gotten to know a few of the members but had not yet received my assignment from God; hence, I had not yet gotten involved in any ministry work. Even though I had always been active in church, I was enjoying just sitting in the congregation and getting fed. In hindsight God was using this time to acclimate me to the needs of the congregation, thus increasing my compassion for those seeking natural manifestation of the rich Word being taught, and illuminating my desire to help motivate, prepare, and equip the saints for the work of the ministry and the edification of the body of Christ. He was solidifying my spiritual formation and stirring up my gifts to be used for His glory, as He told me He would before I left Kentucky.

The second week of December things really began to open up for me. I not only received a full-time teaching contract at John Burroughs Middle School but I joined The City. After three months of feasting on His Word, the Holy Spirit nudged me to let me know that it was time to do more. I had been trained that it was protocol to present one's self to the Shepherd of the House and submit your ministry gifts under his direction. As God would have it, to my surprise just when I decided to do this my former pastor, Dr. Malone, was our guest preacher. During praise and worship he saw me in the congregation and smiled. Before he gave his message he acknowledged a couple and me as former members of his congregation at Canaan. As I knew he would, he delivered a power-packed, spirit-filled message. After service I went up to speak to him. He formerly introduced me to Bishop and said, "Now Bishop, Dr. Cobb was one of my faithful members at Canaan and she's a good worker, so you take good care of her." Bishop responded, "Oh yes, yes of course." I could not let this opportunity pass me by, so I told Bishop I had been trying to set up an appointment to meet with him, but to no avail. He gave me his administrative assistant's cell number and told me to call her.

After several more unsuccessful attempts to get a meeting with the Pastor, I sent him the following letter:

Dear Bishop:

First, I want to thank you for taking the time to read this letter. Because it has been very difficult to arrange a meeting with you, I decided to introduce myself to you on paper. As you know, I have come from Canaan Christian Church, Louisville, KY under the spiritual tutelage of the Reverend, Dr. Walter Malone, Jr. After visiting various churches in the L.A. area, God led me to join your flock in December 2003. Though the Word was being brought forth at each House I visited, it was only under your fervent and compassionate teachings that I was getting fed both spiritually and intellectually. Pastor, I praise God for you!

Second, I want to share with you past ministries in which God placed me to do His work. As a five-year disciple at Canaan, one of the first classes I took after New Members was Spiritual Gifts. My top five gifts were identified as leadership, administration, teaching, exhortation, and mercy. While at Canaan, God enabled me to develop a study guide I used to teach an elective Sunday school class on Leadership. For our leadership team that consisted of all ministry leaders, I also facilitated biblically based workshops on team-building skills, interpersonal communication, and what I coined as 'total quality ministry' strategic planning sessions. I led relational communication sessions at our choir retreat, served in the capacity of Director of the Young Adult Ministry and of the SANKOFA Ministry, as well as developed a curriculum guide for Canaan Community Development Corporation's after-school program.

Pastor, I disclose all of this merely to share with you what God has equipped me to do for His glory. As a people-oriented, purpose-led believer, I know that I have been sent to The City at this appointed time to serve under your leadership. Because I understand the nature of the journey I am on and the sacrifices of the people on whose shoulders on which I stand, I passionately embrace Luke 12:48(b), "For unto whomsoever much is given, of him shall much be required".

Subsequently, as God has instructed me, I humbly offer whatever knowledge, skills, talents, and gifts He has deposited in me to assist in any ministry in which you assign me. Pastor, God knows my heart; I did not come seeking a title or position. I have simply come to roll up my sleeves and take up Jesus' towel of Servanthood to help meet the needs of those who are hurting and in search of wholeness as I was.

I have enclosed a resume for your review. Again, thank you for this time and I look forward to hearing from you to set up a meeting.

Agape,
Carole A. Cobb, Ph.D.

Shortly after I sent the letter, there was a church announcement calling for volunteers to join the Youth and Young Adult Ministry (YAM). While I had no plans to serve in that particular ministry that soon changed after the Word came forth. Just before Pastor preached, someone suggested that I sign up since I had had experience working with youth and young adults before. Somewhat like Gideon, I told her, "Though I love my job, I work with youth all day and I have served in YAM before. I don't know if that's where I want to be. If the LORD wants me to serve in that particular ministry, He will have to tell me. I am not moving until then". Well, He did. Pastor's message was on how we all stood on the shoulders of others and as children of God were required to use our gifts, talents, and abilities to give back. And as believers we could not sit in the pews and be benchwarmers if we had a skill-set that could benefit the Kingdom. As Christians we have to get involved.

God will always send confirmation when He wants us to move. At the end of the message my look told her, "Don't say a word." I knew what I had to do, so I signed up to assist. I decided I would work with the church's middle school youth, since this was the age group I was teaching. Again, as God would have it, those positions had just been filled; however, the Young Adult Ministry was still in need of volunteers and a Director. During my interview I was asked to become the Director of YAM, even though I had only wanted to assist in its development, not lead it. After some deliberation, I agreed to accept the position on a short-term basis. Over the next three years I served on the New Members' Curriculum Committee, and the Los Angeles Institute for Leadership and Ministry Board (LAILM); taught leadership classes at LAILM; trained teachers in the Master Life Series for the Discipleship Classes; and authored the New Members' Manual, "Fresh Start". I was (am) the Morning Host for the Back-2-School Program put on once a year by Ms. Dorean Edwards/CEO Consultant Entertainment.

In addition to serving in the church, I had an incredible experience living and serving in the transitional home. God used me to minister and act as a mentor to two of the women there. As a result, one quit smoking and the other started attending church on a regular basis.

By June 2004, I was ready to move into my own place. I was only able to find a quaint, yet stylish 2-bedroom/2-bath apartment. I took it, even though I knew all my belongings in my KY storage unit would not fit. While in KY, God had greatly blessed me with a beautiful twenty-eight square foot 3-bedroom/2-bath ranch-style brick home that included a living room, dining room, kitchen, and a family room. Downstairs I had a full-sized, fully furnished basement with a utility room, a walk-in cedar closet, and a half-bath. My outside storage unit, adjacent to the two-car garage, was full of lawn care equipment while my yard was home to an eight-piece patio set and a three-tier gas grill. Before heading to L.A. I had given away all of my outdoor furniture/equipment and some of my household belongs, but still had a lot of "stuff" left.

After getting settled in my place, I began recruiting for the ministry. I wanted to establish a Young Adult Advisory Council because my goal was for the young adults to actually run their own ministry while the Council operated as advisors. We interviewed a young man by the name of DeJon who had a strong presence about him. During the interview he shared some wonderful ideas for the growth of the ministry that had elements of what I had envisioned. We selected him and several others to form this Council.

Over the course of time, as we were planning the role and the structure of the Council, he and I developed a solid friendship; he had become like a brother to me. We often called each other after service and discussed the message Pastor had delivered. We sometimes met before Wednesday night Bible Study, which is when I found out that he was a prophet. DeJon would actually convey to me the essence of what Pastor was going to talk about during service. He was right on point every time! I had never encountered anyone with this degree of giftedness.

It was now the end of August. During one of our discussions, something the Holy Spirit had told me before coming to L.A. came back to my memory, "... I now want you to use all of your gifts, talents, skills, and abilities that you have used in the world for the expansion of my Kingdom." Because the ideas that DeJon and I were sharing were incredibly parallel, we decided to merge them and create several plans. On a couple of occasions we presented these plans to the church leadership, but they were reluctant to embrace them. I later learned that several years ago, DeJon had left an unfavorable impression with the church stemming from his dishonorable treatment of some of the members. They just did not trust him. However, believing in the ministry of reconciliation, I wanted to give him another chance. After all, God is a God of many chances and He has given us all quite a few.

Making no headway we began talking about forming a partnership to do the work of our ministry. We began spending even more hours on the phone and often meeting after work to iron out the logistics. Before we could jointly fit the visions God had given each of us, we had to first create an infrastructure that could support the ideas as we strategically wove them together. In our planning I saw the hand of God moving in my life as I was directed by the Holy Spirit (through one of Bishop's sermons) to gather all the ideas and programs I had written over the years and dust them off. In the greater scheme of things they would all fit into what we were creating for the Kingdom.

By September I had found a huge house with a bedroom and a bath on the west end and a bedroom and bath on the east end. It had a nice size living room with a separate den, a kitchen and a utility room. I had sufficient space for all of my stuff that was still in KY. It seemed that after a year, it was finally time for me to get settled into my new home. DeJon lived in Pasadena and we had both agreed that the hours we spent on the phone could be better used if we lived closer. He asked me if I was looking for a roommate and I told him I was fine living by myself. He went on to ask if he could become my roommate anyway, something I didn't see coming. I thought about it for a while, and after asking some real personal questions about his past, I agreed to it. This was another first for me. I had never had a male as a roommate, but because the relationship he and I had was purely platonic and focused on Kingdom business, I had no real concerns. Besides that, he was not at all physically attractive to me, so I said yes.

By now, I had become disenchanted with the educational system and was at a point in my life where I wanted to see change, real substantive change in teacher practice and student achievement. I was tired of hearing the same forty-year old problems concerning the miseducation of our children, especially when we knew what changes needed to happen to save them. I just wanted the educators to have the will to put into practice instructional strategies they knew would equip our children for academic success. I wanted the saints to break free of their strongholds so they could operate in their gifts and receive the promises of God for their lives. Juxtapose my professional dissatisfaction to my dismay of seeing people at church stuck in a personal conundrum, even after hearing a rich Word weekly, but not able to apply it to their lives – I was ready to do something. I knew I had the skill-set and was spiritually equipped to help both, but both would require my full attention.

I was truly at a crossroads in my life. Over time we were putting eight or more hours a day into the building of our vision. This pace was becoming physically taxing and I knew I could not continue working two full time jobs. It was my teaching job that was paying the bills but it was the partnership that aligned with my spiritual vision. My spirit was not at peace so I sought God for an answer and He replied, "I did not bring you 2,100 miles to do the same thing you were doing in KY. I am not a part-time God and I need you to serve me full-time". I took this to mean that I had to make a choice, either work for the Kingdom system or for the world system. Because I wanted to stay in His will, the answer was a no-brainer; I chose to work for the Kingdom system.

Ironically, the next day after I had heard God's voice, DeJon came to me and said that because of the magnitude of this vision I would have to make a choice, to either give my full attention to our efforts or he would have to find another partner. After reflecting on what God had just told me, and wanting to be obedient to Him, I knew what I had to do concerning LAUSD. In November 2004, one year after God had placed me there, after giving them a two-week notice, I resigned from my job. This would mean no sure income except what I would earn teaching one class at the Bible Institute. Since I had experienced financial scarcity before, and I knew God to be a keeper, I was determined to step out on faith no matter the cost. I just wanted to help expand God's Kingdom as He had instructed me, which was truly my heart's desire.

The Nugget: *Like David, encourage yourself. Remember that every time God moves you to a new place, He moves with you.*

Obedience Is A Reflection Of Faith.

Chapter Five

Isolation

———

> *"I know both how to be abased, and I know how to abound. Everywhere and in all things I have learned both to be full and to be hungry, both to abound and to suffer need",*
> *Philippians 4:12.*

There was no turning back. I had just a little bit of working capital saved but now I was free to devote all of my hours to Kingdom business. DeJon and I forged ahead with our plans and established a nonprofit public benefit corporation exclusively for public, charitable, religious, educational, and scientific purposes. The specific purpose of this corporation was to develop and/or support projects that empowered individuals and communities through non-partisan research, education, economic development, management principles, and informational activities that would significantly enhance their life experiences and lead them to self-sufficient and spiritually mature behaviors.

Though I can't give you all of the details, our overarching goal was to establish delivery channels that would bring provision to the visions of adult believers who, for various reasons, had not yet experienced the manifestation of their dreams. We had created an 'In-the-House' kingdom-building plan that would link disciples as a community of people through use of their spiritual gifts, vocational skills, and natural talents – drawing on all good works. Having no lack, every person, every family, and every community would enjoy the fruits of our common prosperity.

For the youth and young adults, we wanted to establish a self-sufficient enterprising ministry that trained them how to become principled-centered spiritual leaders who were virtuous, filled with the Word, and empowered Disciples of Christ. Our plan was to give birth to a ministry that was run *'by youth for youth'* resulting in a spiritual, psychological, and economic transformation in their lives. Our ultimate goal was to create positive experiences for youth/young adults to reach their full potential in all facets of business management, technology, and edutainment entrepreneurships. Our church was to be the launching pad of this global mission. With the groundwork laid, our next two challenges were to: 1) identify companies for collaborative partnerships that we felt would support our vision with a financial seed; and 2) create employment opportunities by recruiting and training key faith-based people from various demographics and geographic locations to run satallite programs.

After two months of researching and making phone calls, we finally made some progress. We met with and made our marketing presentation to three companies that were interested. Because we would eventually be applying for federal and state funds that had been set aside for faith-based initiatives, we needed to incorporate a strategy by which to measure/evaluate the success of our efforts. The company we chose was a perfect fit. It already had an unbeaten thirty-year track record, both nationally and internationally, and had developed a wonderful assessment tool we could use to establish benchmarks for success.

As we continued to make headway, we brought DeJon's 'fiancée', DeVonna, on board to help out with some of the logistics. She worked for a law firm and was very knowledgeable in the areas in which we needed assistance. I met her at church and we all went out to eat on several occasions. She even volunteered to help at one of our youth functions. We couldn't afford to pay anyone, so it seemed to be a good fit. In December, he informed me that he was going to move in with her, but that the business partnership would continue as planned. I actually had no problem with this because this meant I would have my space back.

Without any steady source of income, I had depleted my savings by-mid January 2005. It was now March and I had received an eviction notice

– another first for me. In February we received a little working capital from our collaborative partner of which DeJon gave me $1,000 to cover some of my personal expenses. Since we were partners, my supposition was that this was half of what he had been given, minus some business expenses. (Not until the next year – after the 1099 form came – did I discover that he had been given a check for $15,000). Still moving in faith, we expanded our vision to include several other mega churches and their communities, and with the promise of more monetary investment from our collaborative partner, we planned a big kick-off event at the L.A. Convention Center to occur in May. We recruited volunteer workers for this event, brought on board a major sponsor to build our website, and held two orientation trainings for the people we had recruited for our satellite stations. Just when we were building momentum, DeJon began to change. He became overbearing and quite haughty.

He brought on Frenda, a friend of his, to be the president of our youth movement. Whenever I took him back to our original mission based on the vision God had given us individually and the plans we had made collectively, he arrogantly responded that the church was too limited; that we would make more money if we took our concept outside of the church walls. Now don't get me wrong; I know ministry is not restricted to the church and its four walls, and that we are to go out into all the nations. However, we are still supposed to be about building God's Kingdom not fortifying our empires. Like the people described in 2 Timothy 3:2-5, they became *"lovers of their own selves, lovers of money, boasters, proud ... unholy ... without self-control ... despisers of good ... traitors, head strong, haughty, lovers of pleasures rather than lovers of God, having a form of godliness but denying the power thereof".*

You know how you know that you know you have done nothing wrong; you have not intentionally mistreated anyone. You did all that you knew to do that was right, yet things went against you and your plans – things over which you had absolutely no control. Well, that is where I was. I felt as though I had committed a crime against myself. What I had helped build for the edification of God's people was being turned into a moneymaking, for-profit endeavor, and God had been edged out. My comfort came from 2 Timothy 3:12-14, *"Yea, and all who desire to live godly in Christ will suffer persecution. But evil men and imposters will grow worse and worse, deceiving and being deceived. But you must continue in the things which you have learned and been assured of, knowing from whom you have learned them".* This gave me the push I needed to keep *faithin' forward.*

DeJon's deceit did not stop there. Taking advantage of his affiliation with me, DeJon was able to recruit and take advantage of other people within the church under false pretenses. He even used Bishop's name on occasion to gain access to places that he normally would not have. After I learned of this, I informed Bishop who soon had that nipped in the bud. To DeJon's dismay, he would later find out that God's Word is real. You simply cannot mistreat God's children and get away with it. I am one of

God's anointed, and the Word clearly tells us to "touch not My anointed; do My prophet no harm". God's gifts are given to us without repentance, but when we misuse those gifts, and go against the Word for worldly gain, there is a heavy price to pay. Word to the wise, you will reap what you sow for "friendship with the world is enmity with God. Whosoever therefore wants to be a friend of the world makes himself the enemy of God" (James 4:4).

In the Book of Galatians, God's Word tells us "a little leaven leavens the whole lump". It goes on to tell us that we have been called to liberty because in the Spirit there is liberty; however, our liberty is freedom in Christ. It is not for us to perpetuate self-rule or to use it as an opportunity for the flesh, which is exactly what DeJon began doing. He conducted several secret discussions with other 'like-minded' individuals to devise an elaborate scheme to take over our collaborative partner's company…when I found out I was appalled! Since I brought them on board, I set up a meeting with Tim, the lead person of the company and shared this with him. Well, they had not had over thirty years of success without being business savvy themselves. Tim had already had DeJon investigated and put up safe guards to prevent any such madness. He wanted to ride this out because he believed in what we were trying to do for the church and the community.

After about a month of trying to keep DeJon true to our original mission, the Holy Spirit had me to totally disengage. It was now May; he had completely shut me out of all that we had built together. There I was with little money, facing eviction, and dealing with betrayal; I was emotionally shaken. However, the one thing that was not shaken was my faith, because I knew God would never leave me nor forsake me. When I remembered what God brought me through at the beginning of my journey, I knew I could trust Him for the now and the future, for His M.O. does not change; His principles remain the same. Because I was unwilling to compromise, I knew that spiritual warfare was about to begin, so I dressed for the occasion. I put on the whole armor of God and declared war against Satan and all his little imps. Though I walked in the flesh, I knew I would not war in the flesh. God assured me that the battle was His, and that I would emerge victorious as long as I stayed focused on Him and not my situation.

Since I had resigned from the District, I would have to wait until the start of the next school year to reapply. Meanwhile, I applied for several positions in surrounding school districts but none where hiring this late in the semester either. In a last ditch effort to stop the eviction; I tried to borrow money from several of my "friends". Only three came through but it wasn't enough to stop the process. It was now the end of June and I had to vacate. Two days before I was to be out of my apartment, I recruited a couple of brothers from the church to move my material possessions into storage. I did not share with them why I was moving because it was not meant for them to know. I hadn't quite wrapped my mind around the fact that I was now 'homeless'. I spent my last night in my place on a mattress set (that I had planned on leaving). While lying there, looking around at the empty space surrounding me, I took an inventory of my life. This room reflected my life; there was nothing visibly tangible, yet it was full – in the mist of my circumstance my soul was at peace. I had made no plans as to where I would go or where I would live; I wasn't afraid of what tomorrow would bring. I knew, in spite of what I was going through, because my motives were pure, I would overcome.

Despite what looked like a setback, I knew God was ever present, holding me in the hollow of His hand, so I just did what I knew to do. I went back to the place where I always found comfort; I went back to His Word. I began to speak His Word over my life that 'His plans were to prosper me and to bring me to an expected end; all things would work together for good to those who love Him and are the called according to His purpose; He wished that I would prosper and be in health even as my soul prospers...' I knew His Word to be true, so I simply refused to lose my praise. I also knew God loved me, and for whatever reason I was going through this, He would turn it to good. As I reflected on what got me through the other rough times in my life, it was easy to remember that my past victories proved God to truly be Jehovah Jireh. I knew that I would be all right so I rested in Him and went to sleep.

The next day was Wednesday, so I decided to go to Bible Study. At the end of service, just as I started to leave, reality hit me hard. I realized I had no place to go! I sat back down bemused as I watched people leaving and the sanctuary becoming increasingly empty. It was as if I was watching someone else's life unfold before me. As I slowly became consciously aware of what was going on, I saw a young lady with whom I had developed a good relationship. Johanne had a caring spirit and we had worked together in various ministry assignments, but had never socialized outside of church. I did not know her circumstances but I put aside my pride, grabbed a hold of the boldness of the Holy Spirit, approached her, and asked if I could stay with her for a couple of nights. I didn't tell her my story just that I had moved out and had not found a place yet. I knew she wasn't expecting this, but with very little hesitation she told me I was welcomed. Since she had two children, she didn't have an extra bedroom but offered me her couch, which I gladly accepted. God showed me that though I was 'homeless' I was not friendless.

After the third day, Johanne realized that I really didn't have any place to go. She graciously opened her home to me for as long as I needed to stay. Talk about a humbling experience, I had never in my entire adult life felt so vulnerable and yet so grateful. Now I knew how the young lady from Canaan must have felt when I opened my home to her in KY. Unpretentiously, with tear-swollen eyes, I thanked her and gave her a loving, heart-felt hug. Over the next couple of months, during my time of reflection, I realized that my choice to resign when I did was premature. Yes, I had sought God about leaving my job, and there is absolutely no doubt that it was God's voice I had heard, but I had not sought Him as to *when* I should leave. I was so ready to get away from the hypocrisy and step into ministry that I had not left room for wisdom, nor had I sought it as James 1:5 tells us to do, "If any of you lacks wisdom, let him ask of God, who gives to all liberally and without reproach and it will be given to him." Instead, even though my motives were unselfish and had come from a pure heart, I allowed my zeal to serve Him get me off course.

After I began to spend even more time with God, seeking His face continuously – which is what He had meant by "not being a part-time God" – I realized that I had inserted *my will* in my decision. As Pastor stated so clearly one Sunday night, the order *has to be* God's will and purpose for my life, followed by my faith, and then my will *behind* my faith. Whenever it is not in that order, everything is out of alignment and there are natural consequences that will follow. Isaiah 55:8 reminded me that *"His thoughts are not my thoughts; nor are my ways His ways, for as the heavens are higher than the earth, so are His ways higher than my ways, and His thoughts than my thoughts."*

In His infinite wisdom and timely fashion, God used Pastor to unveil this revelation to me. He laid out the overview that Sunday morning and followed it so perfectly with a set of prolific directives that Sunday night and I got it! Along my purpose-led journey to the destiny that God set for me, He also planned a detour that was not seen on *my* map. He gave me an unexpected assignment – to assist DeJon with his vision, for what you make happen for others, God will make happen for you. However, once God gives us a vision we have to be true to it. When we choose to use the gifts He has given us for our financial gain, and not for His glory, there is a heavy price to pay. I had done all I was supposed to do concerning DeJon; it was DeJon who had compromised.

While I was in this refiner's fire, God expanded me upwardly and outwardly. Though I was never alone, it was a lonely but necessary situation. He took me through a mental and spiritual process of purification that confirmed *my* areas of strength and revealed *my* areas of weakness. God used this conflict to expose DeJon and his cohorts as well as to fortify a Christ-like character in me; He showed Himself faithful. Under no circumstance was I going to permit anyone from permanently distracting or keeping me from being obedient to the Spirit. This process helped me to define and shore up what I believed and in whom I believed.

Shortly after my move, God introduced me to another young man in church; this would prove to be a divine setup. Dre worked at the church serving on Bishop's security team and often sat on the end seat of the front row. I sat on the end seat of the second row, so quite naturally we spoke when he came to his post. During offering, he always seemed to need an ink pen to write on his envelope. It came to a point that, when it was offering time, I had an ink pen waiting for him. This began our friendship. I enjoyed watching him trying to keep his praise under control during service. It was good to see that Bishop had a man of God looking out for him. The only time I saw him other than during service was in the lobby before service and when I met with Bishop in his office after service. Dre was always on his post.

Two months had past since I moved in with Johanne and her children and I had not found a job; I was either two qualified or didn't have enough experience in a particular field. In September, after the school year began, I reapplied to the District but had to wait until 'norm' day before I could qualify for a contract position. I was still receiving the small stipend for teaching at the bible institute. Though times were lean, I had enough to keep gas in my car, pay my storage bill, and contribute to groceries...*and I continued to tithe* from what I had. I refused to get discouraged for I knew my God to be El Shaddai, the all-sufficient one and supplier of all my needs, in whom there is no lack. I just had to stay the course and maintain the right attitude while going through the process. Like the Hebrew boys before being put in the fiery furnace, I had a choice to make. I knew that the LORD would be with me, come what may, and that He would perform the word of His servant.

From the teachings of Dr. Dollar, I understood that until I talked it, I couldn't take it. I had to give my spiritual victory a voice, for the angels had to hear it in order to hearken and make a way. I had to publish it publicly; I couldn't just think it and speak it. I had to act on it with faith-corresponding action, because God not only listens to our words, He weighs our actions. For five months, having no place to call my own, I slept on the couch; nonetheless, I had to *convey* actions of prosperity. I could not look poor or broke because my Father is rich in houses and land, and I am his daughter, an heir to the throne. Subsequently, I purposed in my heart that I would not be stuck in Lo Debar forever. However, while I was there, I would show the adversary that I would not be defeated.

Even though I didn't have a lot materialistically, I took Suzan Taylor's advice and attended to the 'self' the world sees. I took extra time out to keep my braids fresh, my fingernails and toenails polished, my attire crisp, and my shoes shined. I let my appearance, language, and praise express abundance; they expressed what I believed. In the canvas of my mind I began to live like I was already prosperous; *faithin' forward* I was already there. My countenance was one of joy and no one knew any differently. The Holy Spirit taught me how to stay the course, speak the Word, and operate as if it had already manifested in my life. As a child of God I declared myself too valuable to allow the enemy to have the victory – I gave him no power, no place, and no presence in my life. I learned to call on the strength that dwelt within me to help me overcome negative attitudes and bouts of frustration. I chose to exchange any negative thoughts for positive ones; to break free from the bondage of yesterday; and find joy in the opportunities that lie ahead of me. I not only deepened my relationship with the Father, I established a nurturing relationship with myself as I chose to continue to believe.

As believers we must keep in mind that our choices will either confirm or compromise our covenant with God. We can choose what kind of attitude and response we will have to our circumstance because choice is an act of the soul; therefore, we each can make choices within our soul. I choose to operate in the peace of God and let Him fight my battles. Charles Swindoll said it so eloquently in his Attitude message:

"The longer I live, the more I realize the impact of attitude on life. Attitude, to me, is more important than facts. It is more important than the past, than education, than money, than circumstances, than failures, than successes, than what other people think or say or do. It is more important than appearance, giftedness, or skill. It will make or break a company... a church... a home. The remarkable thing is we have a choice every day regarding the attitude we will embrace for that day. We cannot change our past. We cannot change the fact that people will act in a certain way. We cannot change the inevitable. The only thing we can do is play on the one string we have, and that is our attitude... I am convinced that life is 10% what happens to me, and 90% how I react to it. And so it is with you... we are in charge of our Attitudes".

The choice is indeed an individual one. When we make our choices, we create our character. No matter what our choices are today, they are ultimately creating our tomorrows. Every choice we make will either cause us to be blessed or stressed; things will either get better or worse. The consequences of our choices – some more deadly than others – will be for our betterment or our bitterness, but we are ultimately responsible for those choices. Subsequently, we can unknowingly become trapped in our own web, unable to break free. It is only when we are able to recognize that we have become entrapped that God can begin processing and preparing us for our journey to freedom.

Understanding what to do after we have sown the seed, prayed the prayer, and turned the faith switch on, is liberating. It is our expectations in each situation that will determine how well we will function while in it, and to what degree of joy we will or will not experience. We are to wait and hope for and expect the LORD to bring us to an expected end. We are to be brave and of good courage and let our hearts be stout and enduring, but make no mistake. While we are waiting and hoping and expecting, we must be busy doing our part.

Even in the midst of submitting and doing our part, habits of mind can sometimes paralyze and delay us from reaching our pinnacle of purpose. The enemy would have us believe that where we are now is where we will always be. I had to decide that I would not empower my past dysfunctions and mistakes to control my NOW. I dug deeply within and remembered that "greater is He who is in me than He who is in the world". God had already revealed to me, through His Word, how I ought to live – in courageous faith, trusting in Him only.

It was in my time of isolation I learned to stand on the integrity of the absolute, infallible Word of God. I realized that God was trying to get the better part of me to come out of me. He wanted me to become one with self – my best self – so I could become an eyewitness for Him. God is always in control, and He creates situations so He can show us who He is. If it had not been for my Wilderness Experience, I would have never known what God was able to do. God wants us to get to know Him, so He takes us through different situations to show us different attributes of Himself. When we are lonely, He's our comforter. When we are sick, He's our healer. When we are vulnerable, He's our protector. When we are weary, He's our strength. When we are stressed, He's our peace. When we are in need, He's our provider. Once we come into the knowledge of who God really is, He expects us to walk with confidence in that knowledge.

Sometimes God has to force us into uncomfortable situations, into a "being" stage of development in order to increase our depth of experiencing and knowing Him. Once I made a decision to walk in the knowledge of who He is, I experienced an upward spiral growth in my *being* and *doing,* whereby my growth in *being* resulted in a higher level of *doing* and an increased depth of service for God. Jesus offers us everything we will ever need to face any situation we will ever face, but it is up to us to decide to receive it. It was within my power to allow what I had *gone through* to frustrate me or to fortify me. I chose to be fortified, for in the midst of this in-between season, my spirit heard the manifestation of an abundance of showers and blessings.

God freed me to continue my pilgrimage to Canaan; to fulfill the visions He gave me before I left KY and journeyed *from there to here*. I so appreciate my isolation, my storms, and struggles, for the purpose of my trials was to reveal more of God to me. My Wilderness Experience was where I learned what true worship was; where I entered into His presence, and there was just God and me…I got a chance to see another view of His Holiness.

The Nugget: *Never give up; this may be your moment for a miracle.*

Protection Is The Direct By-Product Of Obedience.

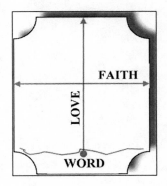

Plant the Word – Grow in Love – Live in Faith

PART THREE: My Promise Land

"Therefore do not cast away your confidence, which has great reward. For you have need of endurance, so that after you have done the will of God, you may receive the promise:"
Hebrews 10:35-36

Chapter Six

Restoration

—∼∽∽—

---

*"To console those who mourn in Zion, to give unto them **beauty for ashes**, the oil of joy for mourning, the garment of praise for the spirit of heaviness, that they may be called trees of righteousness, the planting of the LORD, that He might be glorified", Isaiah 61:3.*

Words of encouragement came to me from Isaiah 51:1-3, "Listen to me, you who pursue righteousness and who seek the LORD: Look to the rock from which you were cut and to the quarry from which you were hewn; look to Abraham, your father, and to Sarah, who gave you birth. When I called him he was but one, and I blessed him and made him many. The LORD will surely comfort Zion and will look with compassion on all her ruins; He will make her deserts like Eden, her wastelands like the garden of the LORD. Joy and gladness will be found in her, thanksgiving and the sound of singing." This was me – in pursuit of righteousness – and I was (am) an heir of Abraham's blessing, so I knew I would find joy and gladness if I fainted not.

I asked myself, "What is it that I love most about God through Jesus Christ?" I found myself answering, "His heart of compassion". Compassion was the keynote of Jesus' life. Wherever He went, He was moved with compassion to heal, deliver, feed, clothe, and restore those in need to wholeness. I have been a recipient of His loving compassion for many years. The Word-seed that was planted in the soil of my heart years ago is what enabled me to stand through my Wilderness Experience and continuously speak those things that were not as though they were. I constantly encouraged myself by remembering what God did for me in past situations. I moved beyond believing to *knowing; I expected* God to restore all. After all, David recovered everything the Amalekites had taken and nothing was missing. He brought back everything and more! God is not a respecter of persons; since He did it for David, I believed He would surely do it for me.

Through it all I developed a healthy attitude of gratitude. I began to give God glory for the things I had and the things I didn't have; for the things I could see and the things I couldn't see. I had no time to stress out any more. Like Paul, I learned to abase and abound, to be content in every situation. I found my rest, my peace, in Jehovah Shalom as I learned to cling to what was good, and to be fervent in spirit 'rejoicing in hope, patient in tribulation, and continue steadfast in prayer'. I decided to look at Abraham, to find out what he was doing *before* the wealth manifested for him. "Against all hope, Abraham in hope believed and so became the father of many nations, just as it had been said to him, 'So shall your offspring be'." Well, I am an offspring of Abraham and, like him I simply refused to consider any thing other than God to be faithful. *Abraham gave glory to God and then God responded.* I decided to follow his example and make thanksgiving a lifestyle.

In late October 2005, the process of financial restoration began. I became a day-to-day sub for LAUSD, which meant I had no control of my assignments and had to go to whatever part of L.A. that needed a sub. Sometimes the distances I had to travel reminded me of the long trek I made from Whittier to L.A. in 2003. Nonetheless, I was grateful to have a job again. Johanne would not take any money from me so I was able to save enough to move out in November. After checking the rental section of the newspaper, I found two possibilities that were in my budget. My first choice had a vacancy for only two nights, which was perfect because I needed two days to gather the documents I needed to submit with my application for the second choice. Even though my credit was shot by now, I received favor from the owner of the extended stay hotel on Grand and 8th and only had to pay $700 a month. Actually it was more like a single-bed hotel room with a small desk, a microwave, a space-saving refrigerator, and a coffee maker. Though it wasn't located in the best of neighborhoods, it was better than I thought it would be. It had a well-lit parking lot, the place was clean, and the front desk personnel were friendly.

The night before I was to move in, my Grand AM was totaled! According to the police's 'mini' report left on my windshield, the incident happened around 6:00 a.m. That morning as I walked toward the car to go to work, I noticed that it seemed to be parked at an angle. The driver who hit my car was going so fast that the impact left the driver side shaped like a 'C'. His car was totaled as well and towed away, but the police did not arrest him because no one was injured. I was infuriated! After various attempts, I finally located him. I wanted his insurance to pay for the damages; my insurance coverage had just lapsed because I didn't have money to continue it. As it turned out, he didn't have insurance either so I ended up renting a car for a month until I could find a nice used one to buy. I didn't like it but this was just another leg of my journey, another test I had to pass, so I continued *faithin-forward*.

I had been in California for just over two years and had no interest in dating, but wanted to get married again. I know this may sound illogical, but what I really mean is that I wasn't going to play the games that too often came with the dating scene. This was my ninth year of celibacy and staying committed to the pledge I made to God. I promised Him that the next man I slept with would be my husband. I struggled the first couple of years and had many chances to break that pledge. However, in my times of weakness, I didn't use any of those man-made devices to satisfy me, I cried out to God for help. I asked Him to take all of those fleshly desires away until I said, "I do", and then redeem the time and give them all back.

Just before the car incident, I had started spending time with a brother I met in church. He was a good-looking gentleman, a nice dresser, attended church regularly, and served in several ministries. We both had been married, so we shared our experiences and talked about expectations in a relationship. I told him early on about my pledge to God, so everything was cool. We'd go out to dinner, catch a movie, hang out at Starbucks, and visit Baskin Robbins, just enjoying each other's company. Sometimes he treated, other times I did. As we spent more time together, I found myself really liking him. All of that changed one day during a conversation we had at dinner; he wanted to become intimate. I must admit, for a second I silently entertained the thought, but then I had a picture of God being there with us, watching us, and being disappointed in me. The Holy Spirit nudged me and the first thing that came out of my mouth was my pledge. As men so often do, he tried to make me believe that men have different needs than women and that it's harder for them to abstain. At the end of the conversation, I told him that God is not a respecter of persons. He is a keeper of those who want to be kept. Needless to say, we never hung out again.

In the midst of my press, the enemy tried to raise his ugly head again. DeJon called me and asked me to "rejoin the team". He left a message on my cell telling me how important I was to the company's success; that if it hadn't been for me they would not be where they were. (I actually kept that message in case I had to use it as leverage later). I took him up on his offer to meet with him to hear him out, but this time I used wisdom. I presented him a list of non-negotiables, and a legal contract with a full description of what my role would be. I knew contract or not, I would have to treat DeJon with extreme caution because he had never shown any remorse for his past actions. I only considered his proposition because my flesh wanted revenge; I wanted to re-coop some of the money he owed me for time and services I had put into the business. Then God said to me, "Don't worry; I've got this". In Romans 12:19 He said, "Dearly beloved, avenge not yourselves, but rather give place unto wrath: for it is written, Vengeance is mine; I will repay, saith the LORD". We met a couple of times afterwards, but there was very little forward progress so I put everything on hold.

December 31st, at the Night Watch service, I received revelation that I passed the test. That following morning, New Years Day, 2006, the Holy Spirit spoke to me and ever so softly said, "Now submit". My immediate response was simply "Yes, LORD" as I fell on my face and began worshipping Him. Whatever He wanted me to do; wherever He wanted me to go; whatever He wanted me to say; whomever He wanted me to serve; I would say "yes" because my soul had said "yes". I was sold out for Christ! I called DeJon, left him a message, and sent him an email to let him know that my season for dealing with him was long over; no amount of money could sway me to return to that madness.

Nothing just happens with God. That second Sunday in January 2006 was the last time Dre attended The City. After service, as I was leaving the church heading for my car, I saw Dre with a sad countenance about him. When I asked him what was wrong, he merely replied, "Just pray for me Doc". Then Dre gave me a hug and spoke prophetically into in my life. He said, "Dr. Cobb, the LORD told me to tell you that He is pleased with you. He said not to worry about anything; you will be all right for He is pleased with you. I just wanted you to know that and to ask you to keep me in your prayers". Though what he had spoken agreed with my spirit, it was so unexpected that it took me a moment to respond. When I did, I told Dre, "Thank you; I received it". I then told him that I would pray for him and his situation. This is when God revealed to me that Dre was His prophet, and he would become my next assignment. I was honored He entrusted me with one of His chosen; however, after the experience I had with DeJon, I wasn't really excited about this. God went on to tell me that unlike DeJon, Dre had a heart after Him and purposed to use his gift to serve the Kingdom. God's assurance calmed my spirit, but I still wasn't quite ready to tell Dre.

During the month of January, the manifestation of God's promises began. I received favor from Ms. Lowe who worked in the sub unit. She saw that I called faithfully everyday for an assignment and willingly took whatever was available. One day she told me to ask for her whenever I called in so she could give me assignments in the area in which I lived. This meant I wouldn't have to drive so far to get to work. The first of February, Ms. Lowe placed me in a high school that had several vacancies. There, I would have a chance at becoming a long-term sub, or maybe even getting a contract.

By this time, God had forged a mentor/mentee relationship between Dre and me – one like Barnabas and Paul. God had assigned me as Dre's divine connection, charged me to give him guidance and insight that would broaden his capacity, challenge him in upward development, and open doors to ministry opportunities. Dre was reaching a crucial point in the development phase of his gift and he had to make some decisions relating to his call. Wanting to stay in the will of God, Dre went on a fast to get some answers.

While on the fast, Dre received the clarity he sought. When he came off, he told me that God had showed him having a great ministry and said to him, "Dr. Cobb will help you". This confirmed what God had told me earlier. This was not something that I had asked for, but I had already told God I would serve whomever He wanted me to serve. Dre's gift was rapidly increasing, but he had not yet learned to manage it. Like an uncut diamond, it needed to be shaped and polished.

Meanwhile, I kept *faithin' forward* by serving on the Special Committee for Education Development at The City. Our charge was to restructure the internal and develop external educational ministries in order to maximize services available to its members. We worked for seven weeks developing systematic, biblically based, Christian education, leadership, and ministerial training programs that would facilitate the spiritual and personal growth of the congregants. Since my background experience and professional training was in education and program development, I took on the task of creating the curriculum for the internal Christian Education department and the external bible institute. In March we were ready to present our proposal to Bishop. The proposal was solid and had all the components he wanted to effectively address the spiritual and personal needs of the congregants. He was impressed and pleasantly surprised by the thoroughness of our efforts. All we needed was his approval to begin implementation in the fall.

In March I also received an unexpected email from one of the schools at which I had previously subbed. I was offered that same position, this time as a fully contracted teacher! God's timing is so perfect. The day I was to start was the day after my 21st day of subbing in that vacant high school position. The significance of this, contractually, was that if you were in the same sub assignment for 21 consecutive days you would get a retroactive increase and placed on a higher sub pay scale. Not only was I eligible for the retro, my teaching contract would be restored with full benefits. The track I was placed on would just be returning, which meant I would have an opportunity to establish the cultural climate I wanted in my classroom. I could create a healthy environment that would welcome my students and encourage them to be and do their best, intellectually and socially.

My greatest desire was for my students to become humane, knowledgeable, and principle-centered adults so I integrated the six pillars of character – trustworthiness, respect, responsibility, fairness, caring, and citizenship – into my content. Each week I identified a famous quote that would govern their mindset for that week. Each Monday as my students entered the classroom they were required to write a response to the quote that awaited them on the board. We would then have a whole class discussion of their responses. At the end of our discussions I always tied the quote and their responses to the lesson for that day.

Whenever they watched a DVD, they watched it with purpose and intentionality. I required them to identify scenes or situations that displayed any of the six pillars of character. Yes, they complained, but I had to keep planting those seeds so they would germinate in their spirits and take root. They had no idea that I was trying to fortify their character and instill in them the will to do the right thing even when it wasn't the popular thing to do.

Though I loved teaching, my intention was not to stay in it, but to move back into administration. At that level I would have the opportunity to positively impact the lives of many more students through their teachers. I would have the opportunity to train teachers in researched-based instructional methodologies and access strategies designed to change their practice and improve student achievement across the board.

As time went on, God continued to restore and shower me with His favor. June 10, 2006, one year after I had been 'homeless' and six months after I had moved into my hotel room, I moved into my own apartment. I had saved enough money to get my household furnishings out of storage and, after almost three years, get my jewelry out of pawn for the last time!

In August an assistant principalship came open at my school, so I applied for it. The interview committee was charged with identifying the top three finalists to be sent to Central Office for a second interview. When I learned that I was among the top three, I was excited and began preparing for the next round. Two weeks passed and I heard nothing, so I made an appointment to speak with the principal. She told me that my name had not been sent forth, and took full responsibility for this. Her defense was, "I know that you will make a great administrator, but we are trying to build a team here. We need someone who will be committed to stay 3 to 5 years, and I don't think you will". This was unfair and she had no right to super-impose her beliefs over the choices of the committee. I respectfully told her that she had violated protocol by what she had done, and even though this school had been my first choice, I would be an administrator somewhere. (Though it didn't happen until the end of the year, I had no doubt that it would).

In September, after submitting a preliminary budget for the bible institute, NJBI, and working out some of the finer details with the attorney and CFO, we were given the green light. As Interim Provost, I wore several hats. I recruited a team of dedicated volunteers and placed an ad in the LA Sentinel and the LA Focus announcing our opening. We ran several announcements in the church programs, passed out flyers, and made announcements before the congregation during all three services for a whole month. I was even given a thirty-minute slot one Wednesday night – to do a PowerPoint presentation about NJBI – during the announcement segment of bible study. We began the registration process for the fall quarter. The Saturday of orientation we had a great turnout. All three instructors gave a seven-minute introduction of themselves and an overview of the class they would be teaching. When the quarter began we actually had thirty-two students enrolled. Our first semester was a huge success. I had to carefully balance my time between my job and ministry.

In October I applied for several other administrative positions similar to ones I held in both Michigan and Kentucky, but was never invited to interview. This was a bit discouraging; nevertheless, I began packing my personal belongs and giving away my classroom materials and supplies. Again, I was *faithin' forward*, preparing for my promotion. In November I decided to give it one more try. I applied for an assistant principal position at another school, and also for a program coordinator at Central Office. This time before submitting either application, I held a conversation with God. I simply said to Him, "Father, this is the last time I am applying. You know my heart's desire is to move into administration. If I am granted an interview I know I will get the job. So I need you to open that door for me. I really want the Central Office position, but I will accept the assistant principalship". Two weeks later I received a 'thanks but no thanks' letter from the school *and* a letter from Central granting me an interview – I was ecstatic!

I was confident in my preparation for the interview but afterwards I felt that I hadn't done my best in presenting myself at the start. The first question I was asked made reference to whether or not I knew the mission statement of the Program. I had not memorized it, so being a little nervous I took the question literally and responded, "No, I do not". I sat there in amazement that this had come out of my mouth, and so did the interview committee. The silence in the room was deafening. After I gained my composure, I proceeded to share with the committee what I did know about the Program. The interview ran smoothly from that point. Afterwards, there was a thirty-minute writing portion I had to complete. The question was reflective of the work I had done for the past twenty years around culturally relevant and responsive education, so I breezed through. Although I left the office with mixed emotions, I still believed God for the position. He was maturing my faith.

On my way home, I called my spiritual brother, Dre. When I shared with him how I began the interview, he laughed in astonishment. I got the same reaction when I told my spiritual sisters, Kavanaugh, Cozzette, and Bev. I couldn't blame them because I had to laugh at myself too. After we regained our composure, I declared that when I get this job, I would be sure to tell everybody that God gave it to me. They all stood in agreement with me. The next day I shared my experience with a dear friend, Dr. Sam, who is a respected minister in the faith. He immediately prayed over the situation, and asked God to give me the desires of my heart because he knew how much I wanted this position. His prayer was very comforting.

The morning of the 9th of December began like most of my Saturdays; this was my time to run personal errands. I picked up my mail from my post office box and decided to go buy a printer cartridge. I pulled into the parking lot of Staples, and before going in, I browsed through my mail. There it was, a letter from the office for which I had interviewed. Before I opened it, I found myself professing, "I know this is not a rejection letter. It is either a letter for a second interview, or a letter confirming my appointment". My heart began to race and my breathing became intensified as I ripped open the envelope. It was dated December 4th. When I got to the third sentence my praise was so loud that the people passing by turned around to see if I was okay. I literally could not control myself, and did not care who saw me or what they thought. I started rejoicing with tears of thanksgiving. I had to give it up, for God had answered my petition!

God's Word teaches us that He is a rewarder of those who diligently seek Him. I frame my world daily with His Words, by speaking my personalized affirmation of verses from Chapters 25 and 37 of the

Book of Psalm. *"Show me Your ways O LORD; Teach me Your paths. Lead me in Your truth and teach me, For You are the God of my salvation. On You I will wait all the day... I will trust in You LORD, and do good; I will dwell in the land, and feed on your faithfulness. I will delight myself also in You LORD, and You will give me the desires of my heart. I will commit my way to you LORD, I will trust also in You, and You shall bring it to pass. You shall bring forth my righteousness as the light, and my justice as the noonday. I will rest in You LORD, and wait patiently for You. For You have promised that if I wait on You, I shall inherit the earth, and shall delight myself in the abundance of Your peace".*

God does things in our lives so we can witness to others about what He did. If we are vigilant, through faith, obedience, and patience, we will receive what God has promised us. When He does show out, we are to give Him the glory, and brag on His goodness to let others know that it was He who caused it to happen, not we ourselves...we only participated.

When we geared up for the 2006 Winter Quarter, we were met with some financial challenges, and management had to make some hard decisions concerning the continuation of NJBI. It had to prioritize projects, and unfortunately NJBI did not make the top-ten list. My supposition is that after analyzing the 'real' cost to run NJBI, and maintain the caliber of instructors I had contracted, management would have to make a major investment of time and money. NJBI was a great idea, but it was just that, an idea and not a vision. Visions are associated with God's plan; ideas are associated with man's plans. Though Bishop is one who loves learning and always encourages the congregation to be life-long learners, NJBI was not a vision, but a good idea. I believe that if Bishop had received a vision from God to establish a bible institute, it would have been a priority, and provisions would have been made to maintain it. As it was, continuation was put on hold.

God has assured us that His word will not return void. Just as He was restoring me, He reached back and dealt with DeJon. Needless to say, the L.A. Convention event never got off the ground, and one year later DeJon and DeVonna had to leave their apartment and move in with Frenda. After three people, from whom they had swindled money, filed criminal charges against them and the company, they spent time in jail. I learned that jail was not foreign to DeJon. His crafty behaviors had landed him there some years earlier. The house they had converted into an office building was totally destroyed by fire, and they eventually filed bankruptcy. I thank God that He had me totally disengage from that toxic situation before I became infected. As Christians we are to confess or acknowledge our sins one to another, and to repent or be woefully sorry before God. DeJon may have repented before the Father, but he still had not shown any remorse for his unethical behavior to those whom he maliciously used. It took some time, but through fasting and much prayer, God healed my hurt and removed my hatred toward DeJon.

I now know that every step of The Journey was meant to awaken me to the power and peace that is mine when I practice cooperating with God. Every remarkable event is a reminder of His glory, that we are divinely protected, but that we must move from living in fear to living in faith. We are constantly reminded that everything works for our highest good, and even though our mind and body may at times be vulnerable, our spirit can never be pierced.

The Nugget: Look inside yourself and learn to walk from the center of who you are in Christ.

By Faith, He Will Restore What The Locusts Have Eaten.

Chapter Seven

Elevation

———∽∾∽———

> *"being confident of this very thing, that He who has begun a good work in you will complete it until the day of Jesus Christ",* Philippians 1:6.

January 5, 2007 I began my new job at Central Office and with this position came new trials. As Program Coordinator I was second in charge, the right hand to the Director who later would become my professional mentor. Some of the Program staff genuinely welcomed me into the family, while others did not. Despite the fact that I had been doing work around culturally responsive and reflective pedagogy for the past twenty years – longer than many of them had been in education – I was "the new kid on the block". Sometimes during our Friday staff meetings, especially those that I ran when the Director wasn't there, a few deliberately challenged my position by trying to dismiss any contributions I offered during our discussions. Some had an attitude because "I had not come through the ranks of the program", while others were upset because the person they hoped would get the position did not. So just like students who test their teachers at the beginning of each school year to determine their resolve, I experienced resistance, and to some degree, disrespect.

It was an uncomfortable position in which to be, but I constantly reminded myself that it was God who placed me there, and no amount of opposition was going to move me. Then I remembered two things: Charles Swindoll's Attitude message, and the fact that we teach people how to treat us by how we treat ourselves. We do this by doing unto others, as we would have them do unto us. I valued myself too much to give control of my behavior to them or anyone else. I treated them all with kindness even when some weren't so kind.

I viewed these opposing forces and negative dispositions as a trick of the enemy, but also as a test from God. Would I respond to their behavior in kind, which would please the adversary, or would I continue to walk from the center of who I was (am) in Christ? I chose the later; I stayed the course. Someone once told me, "All things are preparing you for God's purpose. The resistance that comes against you makes you stronger and builds Christ-like character". I still hold to this belief today. Through this 'initiation' period, every day I declared that *"no weapon formed against me shall prosper"*, and determined in my mind, that as Christ's ambassador, my countenance would reflect Him no matter where I was or with whom I was dealing. I had gone through too much not to have the victory in this situation. I knew that by walking in the spirit the atmosphere would have to change – even though a couple of times I had to 'turn over the table in the temple'. With the power of the Holy Spirit operating through me, I was able to stand steadfast and unmovable. Most of these strongholds have since been broken and we now work together as colleagues in a cooperative and communal environment.

By mid-January God finally released me from my assignment at The City. When the Holy Spirit gave me permission "to shake the dust off my feet" and move on, I was able to exhale. I hadn't realized how heavy this ministerial burden had become. I felt as though a weight had been lifted, and I could now begin a new chapter in my life, only to realize later that God would use this experience as a significant part of my preparation for the next stage of my faith journey.

Things began to manifest quickly and I was reminded of the instructions and the promises God had whispered to me before leaving my home in Louisville. In February I was able to purchase a new car, even though my FICA score had dropped and wasn't what I wanted it to be. In March, while talking to one of my spiritual sisters, I received a divine revelation, but before proceeding, please allow me to digress for just a moment. In Chapter 4, I wrote about my August '03 Faith Journey Celebration and Rev. Dianne prophesying to me that I would have a school. She didn't have many details, but shared what the LORD had given her. Though my spirit bore witness to her prophecy, I did not dwell on it, but quietly processed it cognitively. I had actually thought about opening my own school, one like Marva Collins', but hadn't done anything to make it happen. I believed that if that's what God wanted me to do, I would in His timing. That was the extent of our conversation and I left it there.

In October 2005 the LORD spoke to me and said, "I want you to open a school for my children". Well, I had just returned to LAUSD as a sub, and for the most part was assigned to middle schools, my favorite age group. So my natural mind told me that God meant He wanted me to start a middle school for the children. I was okay with that because that would be my opportunity to establish a school where I could choose my staff and my curriculum focus. My school would have a caring, nurturing, and culturally enriched communal learning environment. It would be a place where all teachers would teach in ways that all children could learn and be able to access core curriculum in order to maximize their God-given potential. The name **APEX** rose up in my spirit; it meant, "pinnacle of purpose". What an awesome name I thought. **APEX** would be a place where students would be equipped with the knowledge needed to walk in their purpose with confidence and power. I was just getting repositioned financially so the school wasn't at the top of my agenda, even though I knew it would happen someday.

Now let's fast-forward 'back' to March 2007. It was not until a conversation with Jae, a friend who worked at The City, was I able to connect the dots from Dianne's prophecy in 2003 to The City's decision not to continue NJBI in 2007. Jae happened to mention that people were still calling and inquiring about when classes would start up again, but she didn't have a definitive answer to give them. Well, I didn't have one either. I told her that I had done all I could do; it was totally out of my hands as to when or if NJBI would continue. The LORD had released me from that assignment and I had moved on to develop my training and consulting firms, Christian Education and Ministry Management (**CEMM**) Group and **TRANSITIONS**. In the middle of our conversation the revelation hit me as to what the LORD had meant two and a half years earlier. "Oh, my God!" I cried. He told me to open a school for His children – not little children – *His* children. As believers, we are His children! My ears of understanding had just popped open, and I heard what the LORD had really meant. He meant for me to start my own bible school. This was so like God; when man closes one door, He opens another – the one He really wanted you to go through in the first place.

The process of establishing NJBI had been my training ground in preparation for creating **APEX** Bible Institute, now **APEX Bible College.** Our tagline is *The Pinnacle of Purpose – where students 'Enter to Learn…Go Out to Serve'*. I fasted and prayed about this because it was going to be a huge undertaking. I knew I could not do it on my own, but I really wasn't supposed to either. The time, God's divine time, had come for me to operate in *moun-tain-moving faith* in order to carry out His directive. I knew He would order my steps and give me the necessary provisions I would need, in fact, He already had. Before God placed me in my administrative position, the salary I made, as a contract teacher was more than enough to meet all of my financial obligations, so I decided to make a covenant with Him. I promised God that I would sow my pay increase into this ministry until He brought sponsorships and grants to **APEX,** and that we would establish a standard of excellence reflective of His nature.

With the audacity to obey Him, by April, **APEX Bible College**, a non-denominational, Christ-centered, educational and training institution, was officially established. With butterflies in my stomach and a prayer on my lips, I sent out mailers and an e-blast to people and churches on my contact lists inviting all to come. The night before we were to have the unveiling, I felt a little like Gideon with the fleece. Although I knew I had heard the voice of God, I prayed to Him and asked Him to put His seal of approval on what I was about to do. Showing His faithfulness, He woke me up around 4 a.m. and told me to read Deuteronomy 4. God had spoken to me many times during the course of this spiritual journey, but that morning, April 15, 2007, was very different. Never before had He given me a specific Scripture to read. Even though I said, "LORD, I don't know what this is about because I hardly ever read Deuteronomy", I rolled out of bed in obedience. I had no idea the confirmation He had in store for me!

As I read Deuteronomy 4, I began to weep uncontrollably with great joy. Over and over again Moses reminded the people of Israel of the statues, the judgments, and the commandments that God had given him to teach them *"lest they forget to teach them to their children and grandchildren to observe that they may live and go in and possess the land that the LORD God of their fathers had given them"*. Well, I was a part of that lineage and it was time for me to go in and possess the land God had promised me as my inheritance, and I did just that! In May 2007, after entering into an agreement with the University of Southern California's (USC) Office of Continuing Education, **APEX** held its first class on its campus. This inaugural class of students is very dear to me and I love each of them like family. They will always have a special place in my heart and in my life.

Now that we are here, I will unashamedly take this opportunity to share with you how, under the guidance of the Holy Spirit, **APEX Bible College** was developed. **APEX** is designed to meet the needs, and respond to the challenges of this new wave of spirit-filled lay leaders, ministers, and pastors who are seeking a more intimate relationship with God. Through practical application of the Word, this broad spectrum of professional leaders and laity engage in dynamic teaching that brings faith and life together, in action. With an uncompromising commitment to excellence, we have created a holistic, balanced curriculum that redefines church, changes lives, connects people, and strengthens communities.

APEX provides a platform where students can discover, develop, and operate in their natural talents and spiritual gifts as they prepare to go in and possess the land God has already given them. We have intentionally merged strong academics with a servant leadership and ministry-driven focus that is based on the incorruptible, infallible Word-seed of God. We welcome both degree and non-degree seekers who have a strong commitment to Jesus Christ; who thirst to walk in their ministerial calling, desire to serve in lay ministry in their church or other faith-based organizations; and/or seek personal growth and spiritual enrichment. Transfer students are welcome at **APEX**; however, only courses in which they have received a C or higher are accepted.

With flexible course scheduling, **APEX** operates on a ten-week quarter system with one additional week for examinations. Certain Modular and Online classes are offered throughout the year. The Bachelor and Master Degrees' Program of Study is Practical Ministry. Students choose from one of the following areas of concentration: Leadership and Ministry Management; Christian Education; Biblical Studies; and Theological Studies. The Diploma Program of Study has concentrations in Urban Ministry, Christian Ministry, and Biblical Counseling. To promote a sense of community within each class, the maximum student-to-faculty ratio that we strive to maintain is 20:1. Students seeking degrees conclude their program with an internship in their area of concentration. Our Personal Development Institutes run four-to-eight week certificate programs ranging from Entrepreneurship 101 to Parenting Skills 101.

Our Vision is a global community of Spirit-led, Godly men and women doing Kingdom Work. Our Mission is to equip, edify, and empower people to become spirit-formed, principle-centered leaders as they find their purpose and destiny by applying God's uncompromising Word for successful everyday living. The core values governing **APEX** are found in **CHRIST** – **C**haracter, **H**oliness, **R**ighteousness, **I**ntegrity, **S**ervanthood, and **T**ruth. We build leaders of commitment not convenience; leaders of character and moral courage, not compromise. At **APEX,** we develop champions for the LORD who reach beyond themselves to build community and a sense of purpose in the lives of others.

All **APEX** faculty have multiple degrees, though faculty recruitment was both a blessing and a challenge. The very first faculty I was blessed to contract was Minister Roxanne, a dear sister in the faith whom I knew to be a living epistle and bible scholar, who taught with great passion and reverence of the Word. When I shared with her my revelation about starting **APEX**, she said that she would love to be a part of this move of God. Then I contracted Minister Marty, a brother in the faith, who had been recommended by a respected colleague. During our conversion, I explained to him our funds were limited but I would pay him a reasonable stipend based on his qualifications. His reply brought tears to my eyes as my spirit bore witness to his sincerity. He said, "Dr. Cobb, I will teach for free. I told God that I wanted to teach at a university, so to have the opportunity to teach on the ground level of **APEX** is an honor". They both have proven to be invaluable assets. I later contacted several other professional scholars who agreed to become a part of this movement.

The challenge came when an instructor, who had taught a class in the non-degree program of NJBI, asked if she could join **APEX**. She had also taught at one of the local bible colleges for six years. Even though I had my reservations, I wanted to give her a chance. After she assured me she knew the subject matter of the class I wanted her to teach, I brought her on board. This decision proved to be a nightmare – I realized that just because one knows a subject, does not mean one can teach that subject. In hindsight, I should have yielded to my reservation – the nudging of the Holy Spirit – and never contracted her. Whenever you are about the Father's business, the adversary is always busy. I literally ended up having to co-plan the course and coach her throughout class. To make amends to my students for my hasty judgment, I offered them a special session to counterbalance her deficiency, and I became teacher of record. I vowed that I would taper my zeal, and never bring anyone else into **APEX** without consulting the Holy Spirit first. I made a covenant with God to be a good steward over what He had given me.

Now, our faculty is a team of seven highly qualified, knowledgeable, and experienced men and women of God who are dedicated to serving our students as they embark on their Kingdom Building

Journey of higher learning. We are now in our second year preparing for, and expecting, the manifestation of God's exponential growth in students and finances. We invite you to become a part of this spiritual movement as a student or as a sponsor. Check us out at our website **www.apexbiblecollege.org** for our admissions policies and forms, registration procedure, complete course offerings, and update or modifications made in our Programs. Though our fees and tuition are comparable to other small colleges, our dedication and service to our students can't be matched.

God had me return to The City in March 2008, one year after leaving. He actually told me a couple of months earlier; I was just waiting for the when. After two of my friends confirmed this, I knew my time was coming soon...it turned out to be Resurrection Sunday (some call it Easter). I was pleasantly surprised to be welcomed so warmly by many of the members. Some made comments relative to the radiance of my countenance, while others discerned my inner peace. I gave all the credit to God for keeping me in His will and showering me with His glory. Then Bishop retold the story of Jesus' death, burial, and resurrection, in a non-traditional manner, as only he could. He said that, in the end, Jesus came back with more power, more anointing, more joy, and more peace! My God, that's how I felt in the spirit! This message was tailored just for me; God was letting me know that He had equipped me for the return.

Loving God, above all else, requires us to serve with humility, and to stay in faith. God had used that year, not only to rejuvenate me physically, and restore me financially, but to elevator me spiritually. As the months passed, I began to understand God's timing for sending me back when He did. He had taken me out to strengthen me so He could send me back in to help strengthen others; to warn against false prophets, break free of strongholds, and illuminate their understanding of what He had in store for them. God had equipped me to stand in the gap for His children, be vigilant on their behalf, and war against the enemy whenever he decided to raise his ugly head. Shortly after my return, DeJon came back. I don't know how long he will be there, but after watching him for a while, I spiritually discerned that he still had a manipulative spirit. When he first returned, he sat in the back during church services. Like a snake true to form, he slowly slithered his way to the front row where he sat when I first met him. My hope is that he will get delivered so that no one else will be deceived by his cunning, deceitful ways. Meanwhile, as long as he and others like him are there, I am to watch and pray.

In the interim, between my restoration and elevation, Dre and I continued about our Father's business. As we studied and prayed together, His spiritual appetite became insatiable as he quickly grew from milk to meat through God's supernatural guidance. The men of God Dre served under were responsible for planting the Word-seed, out of blind obedience I watered, and God gave the increase. It was God who was preparing him to walk worthy of his calling, into the five-fold ministry for which he was predestined. God began this process by elevating Dre into the Office of a Prophet; He later made available several ministry opportunities for him to begin exercising his preaching gift. God then called me into the Office of a Teacher. One evening, as I was watching a minister on TV teaching his flock, I clearly heard God tell me, "This is what I want you to do, teach my Word", reminding me of what He told me He wanted me to do before I left KY. Without hesitation, I told Him, "I will be honored". I have since begun my post-doctoral study in Leadership and Christian Ministry. So that I can be effective in this office, God stepped up my spiritual regiment by intensifying my gifts of spiritual wisdom and knowledge.

Like any brother and sister, Dre and I had disagreements, but we learned to reason together. One topic of contention was school. As Dre learned to manage his gift of prophecy, he became very sensitive to the Spirit. Even though he could tap in and receive direct downloads, I knew he still needed to go back to school. God wanted Dre groomed for greatness; as a prophet to the nations, he would speak before hundreds of thousands, from laity to royalty. In order to be able to flow freely along this continuum, he would have to put in the work. He would need to diligently study to show himself approved.

Dre had almost completed his Associate Degree in Administration of Justice. He often talked about finishing it, but he kept allowing one thing after another to get in his way, primarily finances. Every so often I would check in with him about his plans. He was torn between finishing his degree, then going to bible school for his bachelors' in Biblical Studies, or just going straight into bible school. He also talked about majoring in a totally different field, one that would prepare him for a future and position him to make money, until he was called into full time ministry. I told him that regardless of his major, he needed to get back in school and at least complete the few general education classes he had left. It wasn't until the Holy Spirit intervened that Dre was able to refocus his priorities. He came to the understanding that it was time for him to begin *faithin' forward*, in one direction or the other, regardless of finances. This is when the adversary got mad. You see, the enemy does not care when we are straddling the fence or being indecisive, but he gets upset when we become obedient to the Spirit. When he couldn't get at Dre directly, he sent family members and "friends" to try to block his forward progress and destroy our relationship, but God said, "Not so". We had become so spiritually entwined and in-tuned with God's purpose for our lives, independent of and dependent on each other, that we could not be moved. We believed the Word we studied and stood fast on it, for the WORD is the final authority.

The Nugget: *The Word has to be active in you before it can be active around you.*

***Relentless Faith Is Courageous
Faith That Endures.***

Chapter Eight

Audacity to Believe

—⌇⌇⌇—

"But also for this very reason, giving all diligence, add to your faith virtue, to virtue knowledge, to knowledge self-control, to self-control perseverance, to perseverance godliness, to godliness brotherly kindness, and to brotherly kindness love. For if these things are yours and abound, you will be neither barren nor unfruitful in the knowledge of our Lord Jesus Christ...Therefore, brethren, be even more diligent to make your call and election sure, for if you do these things you will never stumble", 2 Peter 1:5-8; 10.

It is the overcoming that prepares you for the elevation. God brought me *from there to here* without a trace of what I had gone through, because I made a covenant with Him that I would not quit. As a seed of Abraham, I believe the same things God promised Abraham are to be mine. My Wilderness Experience was a place designed to transition me from walking in the flesh to walking in the spirit. I had to be moved from one level of faith and spiritual maturity to another in preparation for handling my inheritance in My Promise Land. "For the promise that he would be the heir of the world was not to Abraham or to his seed through the law, but through the righteousness of faith. Therefore, it is of faith that it might be according to grace, so that the promise might be sure to all the seed, not only to those who are of the law, but also to those who are of the faith of Abraham, who is the father of us all," Romans 8:13; 16.

Hebrews 11 enshrines men and women of faith who triumphed in their own lifetimes, who having obtained a good testimony died in faith, did not receive the tangible fulfillment of God's promise. "By faith Abel offered to God a more excellent sacrifice than Cain through which he obtained witness that he was righteous; by faith Enoch was taken away so that he did not see death; by faith Noah, being divinely warned of things not yet seen, moved with godly fear; by faith Abraham obeyed when he was called to go out to the place where he would receive as an inheritance; by faith, he dwelt in the land of promise as in a foreign country; by faith Sarah herself also received strength to conceive seed, and she bore a child when she was well past child-bearing age; by faith Abraham, when tested, offered up Isaac his only begotten son; by faith Isaac blessed Jacob and Esau concerning things to come; by faith Jacob, when he was dying, blessed each of the sons of Joseph, and worshiped; by faith Joseph, when he was dying, made mention of the departure of the children of Israel, and gave instructions concerning his bones.

By faith Moses, when he was born, was hidden three months by his parents; by faith Moses, when he became of age, refused to be called the son of Pharaoh's daughter, choosing rather to suffer affliction with the people of God than to enjoy the passing pleasures of sin; by faith he forsook Egypt, not fearing the wrath of the king; by faith he kept the Passover and the sprinkling of blood; by faith they passed through the Red Sea as by dry land, whereas the Egyptians, attempting to do so, were drowned; by faith, the walls of Jericho fell down after they were encircled for seven days; by faith the harlot Rahab did not perish with those who did not believe, when she had received the spies with peace...and more. By faith, they all overcame. Therefore, we also, since we are surrounded by so great a cloud of witnesses, let us lay aside every weight, and the sin, which so easily ensnares us, and let us run with endurance the race that is set before us, looking unto Jesus, the author and finisher of our faith." By faith, a young man by the name of Barack Hussein Obama believed the seed that was planted in him before birth, and then watered by his mother and grandparents. Against all odds, He had the audacity to hope. As he continued *faithin' forward,* with Michelle at his side, he became our countries' 44th President and the first African-American to receive such favor.

I, too, was *born by God's purpose for God's purpose*. All of my encounters, while on this journey, were God's way of increasing my faith and my capacity to minister to diverse people across the world to whom He would assign me. Chosen to be a leader of leaders, I had to go beyond hearing and doing to *becoming* ministry. When Jesus was shaping the leaders of the early church, He wanted the tapestry of their lives and ministries to reflect the solid integration of *communion* with God, *community* with one another, and *commissioning* to live in the world but not of the world. As believers, God wants us to grow spiritually. He wants us to become more intimate with Him as we become leaders who, like the apostle Paul with Timothy, can and will teach others how to be leaders.

What one does is the result of what one believes; hence, we are to operate in our God-given purposes, individually and collectively, everywhere we go. With relentless faith, we are to go into the marketplaces where we shop; the environments in which we work; the organizations to which we belong; the families to which we were born; the circle of friends with whom we associate; the neighborhoods and communities in which we live; and the nations we visit – all to demonstrate what and for whom we really stand. But our stance has to be one of tenacity, confidence, and holy boldness.

Living a life that is different is one of the challenges of the children of God, and one that is worthy to be taken seriously. The Bible instructs us to "...seek first the kingdom of God and His righteousness, and all these things shall be added to you". Subsequently, as believers we can no longer afford to operate in the world system as carnal Christians in pursuit of narrow purposes. We must choose to continuously operate in the Kingdom System with a Kingdom agenda. We must choose to create and maintain a platform that not only saves souls, but also delivers and heals them. We must choose to nurture these souls so they may experience God and learn how to cultivate their relationship once they have experienced Him. We must choose to be *living epistles* when we are not on center stage, reaching those who are searching for realism in Christ. We must choose to live the Life behind the Word daily because there is a whole generation looking and thirsting to see this kind of faith demonstrated.

I have learned that in the very hour I ask and believe, it is done, if I have faith and do not doubt. It may not manifest immediately in the natural, but it is done in the spirit. Whatever God says, believe it. There is no room to doubt, for faith is understood to be timeless and boundless. If you believe, no doubt or fear can move you when you have a word for where you are. But don't just have faith, be faithful to what God has given you or told you to do, for faith is the substance of things to come and not yet seen. As you operate in uncommon faith, you shall be blessed and abound in success more than you could ever ask or think, for "the blessing of the LORD makes one rich, and He adds no sorrow with it" (Proverbs 10:22).

Since I began this journey, *from there to here*, I have refused to take the path of least resistance.

Instead, I have built my life on a bedrock of spiritual and personal integrity. I will not practice situational ethics, regardless of what others do, but I will continue to do the right thing because it's the right thing to do. Through Christ who strengthens me, I will always stand morally upright, demonstrate good character, and maintain my honor and virtue in every situation. I have become a faithful giver and an encourager of men and women; pouring into their lives substance that produces lasting results in all areas: spiritual and moral; finance and career; family and home; social and cultural; physical and health; and psychological and educational. I must continuously pay forward; believing that the seeds of investment I plant will touch the lives of generations not yet born.

William James said, "We can alter our lives by altering our attitudes; thusly changing our situations through thought, speech, and behavior, positively impacting the lives of individuals, families, and communities". I am now living my life with an unselfish and unwavering desire to serve others by helping them reach their "pinnacle of purpose". For many, 'what' they need to do in order to maximize their potential is obvious; it is the 'how' that is the challenge. The keystone of attainment is exercising one's gifts by *faithin' forward* – the intersection of belief and trust. This is the place where God overlays His super on your natural, giving you the ability to cause whatever godly desires you have in your heart to come to pass. Faith gives us expectancy to prevail; it produces resistance to the doubt. If you take the first step by faith, God has already taken the next two. God takes great joy when we approach Him with holy boldness and conviction. Even when you are in the mist of your circumstance allow your faith to lift you up. Anchor yourself in God's Word…walk like you have already won!

Be determined; determined people, with a Christ-like mindset, *expect* to succeed. Meet every challenge that comes your way with the boldness of Christ. Expect the best no matter what; either God allowed it or you simply messed up. Nonetheless, as long as you are still breathing, you have an opportunity to go to God so He can turn your mess into a message.

Earlier in my book, I asked a question of myself – Do I really see myself as God sees me? The answer now is unequivocally yes! I finally realized that because I am a 'peculiar people', I should expect peculiar situations. Like David and Joseph, by *faithin' forward* I will come out in an exceptional way, with exceptional victories, because I serve an exceptional God, who is able to deliver me in an exceptional fashion.

I have the audacity to believe that God will orchestrate every dream in my life, because my dreams came from Him! The dreams He gave me revolutionized my present by introducing the depth of my life to the pinnacle of my purpose. As one of God's Generals, I am a change agent predestined for greatness. The visions He has given me are designed to transform the atmosphere in which I walk, in order to meet a need that will bless many and alter the course of humanity for His glory. This is not arrogance, but godly confidence in the divine power of the Holy Spirit who resides in me, and faith in the promises He has revealed to me; for the just shall live by faith.

In the midst of my transition, I did not understand what God was up to; all I knew was that it was uncomfortable. I said to Him, "Father, I really don't like this, so You will have to give me grace to bear it until I get to the other side of it". He didn't change my circumstance immediately, but He did change *me* in my circumstance. God had to get me to a place where I understood that everything I saw was the result of everything I didn't see. I learned that it was alright to ask God a question, but it was not alright to question God. Just trust that His invisible will always conquer your visible.

If you remember nothing else from this book, please remember this: *"'The fear of the LORD is the beginning of wisdom, and the knowledge of the Holy One is understanding' (Proverbs 9:10). All that you do should be done under the governance and the reverence of the Father, for there is no want to those who fear Him. When you are truly in righteousness, no matter what happens, nothing that comes against you will move you. In the end, it will be your character, your integrity, and your lifestyle God will remember, not how intellectual you sounded or how well you articulated a message. When we allow God to order our steps, to operate in the supernatural on our behalf, then the journey is no longer a struggle. When we allow the Holy Spirit to 'undo' who we are in the natural, it is transforming; old things pass away and all things become new. However, we must dedicate our lives to this change on a daily basis. We have to be faithful to 'the who' God is making us over to be. We have to submit our mind, heart, and our spirit to Him – in total obedience"*

Don't grow weary in well doing, for in due season you shall reap, if you faint not. Believe God has a plan just for you and that He is strategic in all His ways. Don't move haphazardly in your own under-standing in getting *from there to here*; operate with a constancy of purpose. Use your spiritual synergy, and have a laser-like focus on where you're headed in life – learn to wait on God, hear from God, obey God, and then maximize who and whose you are for His glory. If you do these things God can and will keep you holy so that you *cross over* to the promise land, and not just *look over* at it as Moses did. You have too much to lose, so remember; faith and fear cannot occupy the same space. Don't be like Peter who stepped out of the boat in faith and walked on water, then took his eyes off Jesus in fear and began to sink. Keep your eyes on where God is taking you...into your promise land.

Minister Eugene was right when he told me that everything and everybody I needed would be waiting for me in California. First, God gave me four Generals to march with me on The Journey *from there to here*. Kavanaugh, an apostle, has been with me on this journey since the beginning. Along the way, God divinely placed in my life a preacher/teacher, Dr. Cozzette, and two prophets, Dr. Bev and Minister Dre. Just as the body is fitly joined, each has been uniquely positioned in my life to encourage, correct, caution, and/or advise me whenever I need it. They cover me and keep my hands lifted when I grow tired. They will continuously help me stay secure and solid in Christ, the one who enables me to take the hits and never be shaken. I am sincerely grateful to each one of them, for each has given me a piece of their heart and welcomed me into their lives.

Second, I must thank God for Horace, my graphic artist, who is not only skilled, but anointed. God sanctioned the writing of this book, so I needed someone with the gift to see my vision for its cover. I saw some work Horace did for one of my students and I asked for his number. During our conversation he said, "I need you to write down what God gave you, as best you can, and I will take it, pray about it, and ask Him to anoint my hands to create it." From his response, in my spirit I knew he was a Godsend. Here's what I wrote, "My thoughts for the cover are simple. I love scenes that evoke a sense of peace and tranquility (without putting people to sleep). I want something soft and peaceful, yet heavenly bound, like a silhouette of the Cross, on a distant hill against a clear blue sky, with a light/glow of countenance illuminating from it. Because the book is about a journey, there has to be a road/path represented but there does not have to be a person on the cover. Trying to make it inviting for all, no matter what their journey is or may have been. Hope this makes sense". As you can see…he saw my vision.

When you have the audacity to believe, you will keep bouncing back because the hand of God is on your life. You don't have to try to veto or over-ride the

Word, *use* the Word and say back to God those things He said to you. He will honor them. Understand the goodness of God, for He is faithful to those who are faithful to Him. Know your birthright; *"you are a chosen generation, a royal priesthood, a holy nation, His own special people, that you may proclaim the praises of Him who called you out of darkness into His marvelous light"*, *(1 Peter 2:9)*. Understand as I do, that as a believer you are an heir of the Father, co-heir with Jesus the Christ. Don't trade your birthright for a bowl of porridge. Remember the promises of God and continuously renew your mind, regenerate your body, and reawaken your spirit through the love and power of Christ Jesus. As you walk in His footsteps, may the riches of our Father be showered upon you today and forever more.

The Nugget: Keep faithin' forward. In Kingdom work, it's about the mission, not the position.

… Enjoy Your Journey …

Stay In Faith…Walk In Destiny!

ABOUT THE AUTHOR

—⟨ꝏ⟩—

D r. Carole A. Cobb is Founder and Provost of **APEX Bible College**, housed on the campus of the University of Southern California (USC). She has created a personal development program entitled *DREAMS: Developing Realistic Expectations through Academics, Mindset, and Service.* Carole is co-owner/developer of Mini Moguls Edutainment which produces a financial literacy comic book series entitled *Mini Moguls: Lessons in Money Management*; and a self-published author of a poetry book entitled *RELATIONSHIPS...the greatest challenge of all.*

A leader of leaders and CEO of two training and consulting firms, Dr. Cobb has developed a synergistic method to capacity building that creates a constancy of purpose within organizations, and promotes a spirit of excellence that changes patterns of thinking and ways of doing. Christian **E**ducation and **M**inistry **M**anagement (**CEMM**) Group provides services to faith-based, and other non-profit organizations, in ministry development, leadership training, community relations, and strategic planning. **TRANSITIONS** provides training to educational institutions in culturally relevant and responsive education, and program development; and change management, leadership development, diversity management, and coalition building to for-profit organizations and community agencies.

For information in regards to securing Carole Cobb for speaking, teaching, training, or consulting, please email her at cemmgroup@msn.com or write to CEMM Group, Suite 361, Los Angeles, CA 90036. You may also visit her website www.carolecobb.org to learn more about her.

Watch for Carole's next book, *The Lone Distance Runner: From A.D.C. to Ph.D.* to be released in 2010. It too will be made available on www.amazon.com, www.barnesandnoble.com, www.borders.com, and www.xulonpress.com, as well as in Target.

Printed in the United States
142499LV00001B/4/P